soul

calling

soul

calling

breathing spirit

into a life of service

julie ruth harley

United Church Press

Cleveland, Ohio

United Church Press, Cleveland, Ohio 44115

© 1998 by Julie Ruth Harley

Printed in the United States of America on acid-free paper

03   02   01   00   99   98   5   4   3   2   1

Library of Congress Cataloging-in-Publication Data

Harley, Julie Ruth, 1960–
     Soul calling : breathing spirit into a life of service / Julie Ruth Harley.
     p. cm.
     Includes bibliographical references.
     ISBN 0-8298-1278-4 (pbk. : alk. paper)
     1. Service (Theology)   2. Spiritual life—Christianity.   I. Title.
BT738. 4. H37   1998
248.8'9—dc21   98-35072
                                                                          CIP

For the people I love

and for the God who, unbelievably,

loves me

Finally, beloved, whatever is true, whatever is honorable, whatever is just, whatever is pure, whatever is pleasing, whatever is commendable, if there is any excellence and if there is anything worthy of praise, think about these things.

—*Philippians 4:8*

Contents

A Prayer of Servanthood

Gracious God, as always, you overturn conventional wisdom about what it is to lead a good life. The world speaks to us in the language of dominance and submission; you call us to be servants. The world tells us to win through intimidation; you call us to seek the good of our neighbor through devotion and humility. The world tells us to be concerned only with building our own nests of personal comfort; you call us to share the cardboard bed of the homeless man and to grip the hand of the woman who wants to die.

How are we to make sense of servanthood in a world of individualism that pulls us away from community and into cocoons? Help us to be bearers of your light in the shadowy places of this broken world. With our program planning, give us compassion to feel the vulnerability of the neglected child. As we review our budget, remind us of the desperation of the frail elderly person on a meager income. While we work through our committee's agenda, help us to remember to treat other people as precious in your sight.

We know as Christ's servants our hands will get dirty. We will feel great pain. We will not always love all the people we serve. Our best-laid plans will undoubtedly have to change. We pray that these sacrifices will be balanced by your blessings: richness of spirit, maturity of vision, and abundant life in your world without end. Amen.

Preface

This book is written about one central challenge in life: How is it possible for us to sustain our own souls while caring for the souls of others? It is a question I have struggled with for many years, a problem that confronts anyone who seeks to live in the model of Christian servant ministry. Wrestling with this issue is not a diversion from the life of Christian service but an invitation to the very heart of it. This book does not promise a solution to the dilemma. It is not merely a how-to book for busy people. It is instead a reflection on the burdens and blessings of trying to help other people.

This book is intended for people in many walks of life who provide care and service to others: nurses, social workers, clergy, educators, students, lawyers, fund-raisers, therapists, volunteers, physicians, retirees, health care workers, parents, executives, chaplains, activists, administrators, doctors, church staff members, missionaries, service employees, and others who have made an intentional commitment to live their lives as an expression of Christian faith. Some of us may be in explicitly religious roles; others' commitment to servanthood may not be publicly recognized. As we go about the work of servanthood, it is assumed that we will know how to nurture and develop our own spirituality. But often we don't. We may have education, training, and experience, and we may have warmed many a church pew in our day, but that doesn't necessarily mean we know how to sustain our spiritual lives.

Soul Calling is written for people who have a strong sense of Christian calling or purpose in the care they provide for others, whether their ministry is lay or ordained, whether their work is paid or unpaid. This book offers reflections on deepening spiritual life while engaging in religious service and is grounded in mainstream Christian theology. It draws upon the rich spiritual resources of the United Church of Christ tradition. I hope these chapters will remind you that you are not alone in the struggle to sustain your soul as you fulfill your vocation.

As Jacob wrestled with the angel prior to crossing the ford of the river Jabbok (Gen. 32:24–31), anyone who is seriously engaged in servanthood will at times resist, surrender, and experience victory and defeat on a spiritual level. This inner wrestling usually has implications for our physical, emotional, and social lives as well, making our soul work crucial to our health and the well-being of our loved ones. Jacob's story from the Hebrew Scriptures teaches us that these times of struggle can be transitions to new life. After cheating his brother, Esau, out of the family blessing, Jacob pursued restoration to his family's love. Seeking to leave behind his painful past, and fearing the upcoming reunion with his estranged brother, Jacob discovered that God did not reject him or close off a future with hope. However, God also did not make Jacob's path an easy one. The literal wrestling match with the angel on the riverbank was an important bridge to Jacob's new life. God seems to believe that such struggles of the soul and testing of the heart will lead us toward greater personal integrity and religious authenticity. Such struggles are also humbling. As Jacob said when he had come to a draw with the angel, "For I have seen God face to face, and yet my life is preserved" (Gen. 32:30).

As Christians, we know the joys of faithful service and also the difficulties of staying focused on our calling. In many ways, serving others can be a crucible for faith, providing a refiner's fire for the soul. Impurities are burned away, and our remaining essence is stronger and more resilient. It is hard work, but it is also good work.

In the chapters of this book, I describe many types of experiences that can threaten our devotion to a life of service. It is a heroic task to integrate servanthood and spiritual life, and I am often amazed that God trusts us to be capable of it. Truly, we have the life of Christ ever before us, we have the good words of Scripture, we have the guidance of other persons of faith, and so much more, and yet at certain moments in our lives the task seems beyond endurance.

My ministry as an ordained pastor in the United Church of Christ is in the field of health and human services, what we call "diakonal ministry" in the church. Its distinctive characteristic is the fusion of care for the body with care for the soul. You will find that many of my illustrations refer to experiences in health and human service ministries, which reflect an extraordinary blend of sacred and secular values. *Diakonia* is one part of the classical definition of the Christian church. The three elements of church life are *kerygma*, the preaching of the gospel; *koinonia*, the community of the faithful; and *diakonia*, the translation of our faith into acts of love and compassion. Each of the three words comes from Koine Greek, the original language of the Christian Scriptures. Throughout this book, I will refer to the work of human care as "diakonal ministry" or "Christian service."

Since 1988 I have served on the pastoral care staff of Lifelink (formerly known as Bensenville Home Society), a United Church of Christ–related organization in the Chicago area. We care for children, families, and older people through a variety of residential and nonresidential programs in more than fifty locations. This is often a heartrending task, and it has brought me into contact with many people living with chronic physical, emotional, and spiritual pain. I have also witnessed remarkable triumphs of spirit and incredible, hope-filled life transformations. I share in this book some of these experiences, although I have changed the names of the persons involved and refer to them only by a fictional first name. The stories of the people we serve are dramatic: children brought from the cribs of overseas orphanages to be adopted into families in the United States; senior citizens who have worked all their lives and yet have little income to sustain them during retirement years; foster children who are alternately wounded and beautifully strong, who have no secure sense of where they belong; nursing home residents who have experienced death in life. Souls like these have posed profound spiritual challenges for me and for others who serve on our staff. They provided the motivation to write this book.

My spiritual life has been formed not only by my ministry, but equally by my life experiences as a wife, mother, family member, and friend. While serving full-time in ministry, I have struggled on a daily basis to be emotionally and spiritually present to loved ones and to maintain a simple home. I have also contended with personal health concerns. In all of the essential parts of life I have been richly blessed, and yet—wishing to savor every good experience that is available to me—at times I rail against the choices I must make about personal investment. I want to give all of my soul to every aspect of my life, but I have realized that this desire often leads to exhaustion. I am learning to understand and accept this. I have come to terms with my sin of pride—believing that I can be all things to all people, that I do not need to rest on the Sabbath as God requires. I have learned to rely upon the support of others and to focus my energies on only one task at a time. Retreats and private prayers help my soul recover equilibrium after I have been deeply involved in some outward concern. Naturally, the more private aspects of my journey are intertwined with my vocational role as servant. There are times when I bring the two together, and there are times when I keep them separate. God has helped me to know the difference.

Acknowledgments

To my wonderful and beautiful family, to every member of the Lifelink community, to my colleagues in the Council for Health and Human Service Ministries, and to my readers—Keith, David, Deborah, Paul, Hal, Ann, and Holly. This is for you.

Introduction

How can we sustain our own souls while caring for the souls of others? How can we allow the Spirit to breathe into our lives of service? The chapters of this book explore and attempt to answer these questions by approaching them in several ways. The inspiration for the first six chapters is taken from a divine meditation by John Donne, a seventeenth-century English clergyman and writer:

> Batter my heart, three person'd God; for you
> As yet but knock, breathe, shine, and seek to mend;
> That I may rise, and stand, o'erthrow me, and bend
> Your force to break, blow, burn, and make me new.[1]

You will learn more about Donne and his Holy Sonnet XIV later in the book. This prayer captures for me the way that God reaches into our souls through the work we do and the lives we lead (our soul calling). Donne's sonnet also expresses the ambivalence we feel about the way that, through our care for others, God tears down old assumptions and creates us anew. We welcome God's gentle approach, the open door, the still, small voice, the healing touch. But we are often unwilling to accept the greater challenges that await. We are bound by powers of sin and evil, and at times God's only avenue to bring us to abundant life is to approach us by force. We come into this work seeking only to help people, and go out with the grim knowledge of our limits. We come in with sweetness and light, and go out in lonely darkness. No one warned us about this God. Yet Donne knows it is this God, too, who can liberate us.

Chapter 1 describes the battered heart, how servanthood affects the soul. We are tested by the tragic experiences laid open for us in the lives of the people, the families, and the communities we serve. How can we bear to watch their sorrow? How does our close contact with real and seeming injustice exact a toll upon us? How can this be woven into the spiritual life without making us cynical or bitter? I offer four principles for those who seek spiritual integrity: finding new definitions of worth; living "in but not of" the system; understanding growth as a means, not an end; and preserving the language of faith.

Chapter 2 poses the question, Whose power is it anyway? We are followers of a Messiah who overturns conventional definitions of power, rejecting notions that power is measured by our net worth. Christ invites us instead to experience power in spiritual ways: through the depth of our commitment to the welfare of others; through encountering Jesus in the people we serve. We are powerful when we recognize that Christ has asked us to serve in his name. We are powerful when we practice humility and when we bear witness to God's power in the world. We are powerful when we respect the integrity and strength of the people we serve. Five elements allow us to uncover the power of Christian service, sustaining us in times when it seems our work does not make a difference: history and the test of experience; prayer; spiritual passion; grief and death; and forgiveness.

Chapter 3 addresses calling and vocation, our motive and purpose as Christian servants. We need to establish with certainty and then rehearse again and again: Why are we here, and what do we hope to accomplish? It is confusing when our original sense of calling or our ultimate goals seem to change. Are we still being faithful to Christ? Why do we not feel the same enthusiasm we once did for our work? How do we respond to spiritual setbacks in healthy or unhealthy ways? Can we accept a life transition as a signal that it is time to reassess our motive and purpose? This chapter encourages us to remember our beginnings and to envision clearly our future goals so that we can best respond to the demands of the present.

Chapter 4 discusses the hard work of the spiritual life and the ways in which we would rather spin into burnout than engage in regular spiritual disciplines. We are exhausted by daily demands and feel that time for prayer and meditation would only be another duty to add to our agenda. We are caught up in secular pressures and lifestyles and allow ourselves to spend little time in intimacy with God. There is meager social support for pursuing an active spiritual life, and the subject goes unaddressed for many, even in a seminary or church environment. We follow the path that leads to professional emptiness, dissipation, and addiction, and see that as somehow a badge of courage. It is, instead, a sad sign of spiritual anemia, the adult soul's equivalent of what we call in neglected infants a "failure to thrive." We can look around and see the consequences of this lack of attention in dispirited clergy and congregations, abuses of power and authority, and Christian institutions that have lost their sense of mission and vision. In contrast, servant-leaders who devote significant time to their spiritual lives can resist the perils of modern life and continue to pursue their commitments with renewed purpose.

Chapter 5 explores holy obedience. Our work demands decisiveness and leadership, yet God demands also that we learn to be obedient followers. Spiritual life challenges us to live on two levels: pursuing our own vision while also following God's purpose for us. We must constantly switch gears from obeying God to leading God's people, and there are times when it seems easier to lead God and follow the people. Even Jesus was tempted to use his power in ways that would have satisfied his followers, but that were not part of God's will. Any of us who say the Prayer of Jesus regularly know the difficulty lies in developing sufficient character and spiritual awareness to know how to lead with holy obedience. It requires listening for the Spirit; practicing humility; resisting evil; and moving forward after pain.

Chapter 6 concerns our need to balance the values of interdependence and individualism. Because we are incomplete as individuals, we depend upon the help and support of others to maintain our spiritual health. Servanthood must be exercised in community, though communities in these times are often created rather than emerging naturally through geographic proximity. Our neighbors may be not down the street, but at the other end of a telephone line. People have different needs and ways of practicing community and autonomy. We are called to learn the rhythm of engagement and retreat, serving at times alone and at times as part of a group, and to lead others to individual achievement, meaningful celebration, and participation in community.

Chapter 7, inspired by John Updike's *Hugging the Shore*, offers practical suggestions to integrate spirituality into a life of service. We pray, but we do not always find a connection between spiritual life and daily work. In our peaceful devotional times and retreats, all seems right with the world, but when we rejoin the messiness of home and work, our inner serenity evaporates. For many of us, spiritual life may be a very private pursuit, something we are uncomfortable about sharing openly. Visible displays of religious belief seem inappropriate in some settings, and there is always the fear of offending someone who does not share the same faith. Can we pray in the workplace? Is that what we are getting paid for? But without devotional times, our work loses significance. If we are to live a life in which the Holy Spirit flows naturally through the center, we cannot put the spiritual life in a box and open it only on special occasions. Rituals and spiritual practices celebrated at work or at home can make any place a sanctuary for the living God.

I have experienced the challenges of blending spirituality and service. My purpose in this book is to tease out the ambiguities presented by serving others and to recommend ways to learn from them. A marathon runner must pay attention to proper rest, diet, and exercise; those of us dedicated to intentional Christian service need to pay attention to prayer, reflection, and community. May this book help you train for the spiritual journey that lies ahead.

≈ **I**

How Servanthood
Affects the Soul

Batter my heart, three person'd God.
—*John Donne*

Servant ministry is work that batters the heart. I hardly need to give examples, for all of us can envision a person at one time in our care who touched us in heart and soul. The sweetness of the love we felt for that child of God came mixed with sorrow for the person's situation in life. As we came to know the person more deeply, as we shared perhaps a secret of our own souls, we felt the battering of the fortress we had built around the deepest self. Our cherished values and beliefs were shaken by the encounter. At times these carefully guarded principles had to be destroyed by the challenge of the other's situation. At other times, with greater inspiration from God, new life and new soul work arose from the ashes of what had to die.

This is the fearsome gift of spirituality in diakonal ministry. It is the voice within that tells us to "go deeper." It is violent, as Donne's poem implies, and we risk that something inside us will be broken and overwhelmed as we allow our spirits to be truly engaged in life. And yet with this risk come growth in God's abundant grace, astonishing possibilities for self-transformation, and the miracle of being able to stand in the holiness and peace of Christ.

≋ Acquainted with Grief

Recently, my heart was battered as I attended a funeral service for one of our longtime Lifelink community members. I had known Trudy as an active volunteer in our nursing home who for fifteen years lived in the subsidized housing residence next door. She was always smiling, friendly, sweet-spirited, and devoted to her church. When her neighbors would complain about the usual things, Trudy did not join in. She had a way of "reframing" problems in a down-to-earth way, always allowing room for a bit of mystery, not feeling that she had to solve everything herself. Though she came from a very traditional European background, Trudy accepted me instantly as a female pastor. I will always remember a compliment she gave me: "I think for a minister you are too beautiful!"

This lovely woman was diagnosed with pancreatic cancer six months before her death, and she spent her last weeks in immense pain. As the pastor conducting her funeral described Trudy's life story, I was amazed to learn about the other challenges she had endured in an earlier part of her life. A German citizen, Trudy was widowed at age thirty when her husband was killed in World War II. She was left on her own with a daughter to raise and decided to come to the United States to start a new life. She worked for years as a seamstress in a Chicago factory to support her child. Only after thirty years was Trudy able to retire and truly "fly free" of this heavy responsibility. She found great happiness in her retirement years and lived with zest, spending much of her time enjoying her grandchildren and serving others. Trudy's final burden came in the form of cancer, which she endured grimly, lying in bed, her skin yellow with jaundice, asking over and over, "Why? I don't understand why this happens to me."

I wept at her funeral for the beauty of this triumphant life, while also feeling very angry about the undeserved pain of her last months. I have known people with more tragic stories. I have seen people experience suffering worse than hers. But knowing the depth of Trudy's struggles helped me appreciate her tenderness, warmth, and humor. I found myself acknowledging that there are times when we think we are serving other people, but in fact they are serving us. This was for me an example of the new wisdom that breaks through to us when we allow ourselves to live in the midst of ambiguity. I did not need to make a decision about the goodness or badness of Trudy's cancer. I did not need to pronounce a judgment of fair or unfair on her life situation. It was not up to me to resolve neatly the messy ambivalences. Putting aside those questions, I was able to acknowledge that the soul of this woman had been a gift to me. The circumstances she encountered, which were part of her story, contributed to her character and the richness of her spirit. It was clear that she had ministered to me in an unexpected and unconventional way. And it was for me an experience of surprising grace.

Those of us who have chosen servanthood as our life path are surrounded by human need. The people we care for may be acutely or chronically ill, have physical, mental, or developmental disabilities, or have problems that stem from one of our many social ills—poverty, racism, sexism, abuse and neglect, homophobia, unemployment, addictions, ageism, and others. I have often wondered why Jesus would call us to such company. Why must we subject ourselves to the terrible questions that these problems bring? Why couldn't Jesus call us to work that is a little bit more fun?

But illness of any kind can be a place of spiritual growth. Sickness makes us shockingly aware of our humanity; it reminds us that we need one another. As one of my colleagues put it, "A healthy person's first brush with serious illness teaches more than all the books written on our vulnerability and need for spirituality. Strangely, it is also then that one tends to feel most abandoned by science, friends, and (yes) God." Those of us who have a modicum of strength are called to be with those who are weak. Our presence and care provide God's mercy to those who are desperately alone. We can rarely enjoy the reason we have been brought together—

because one of us is homeless, dying, or developmentally delayed—
but we can appreciate that there is something essentially human
and deeply religious in our encounter. A world without vulnerability would be a world without compassion.

Coming to terms with contradictions like these is hard. Besides
shedding tears, what can we do? Sometimes nothing could be more
important than our tears. As Christian servants, we are called to a
ministry of human care. By necessity, our lives are not always filled
with light and laughter. We are brought into close contact with
death, suffering, injustice, and the anger we feel at each of these.
We feel worn down, underpaid, and unappreciated, and we wonder
at times why the very people we are trying to help are the ones who
set up obstacles to our progress and their own. Jesus' "little ones"
seem quite unappealing at times. Our tears may be a lament for the
suffering of others, but they may also be an outlet for some of our
frustrations.

God must be the one to batter our defenses, for we naturally
work hard at self-protection. Our hearts grow dangerously vulnerable if we become too close to the people we serve. If we love them
too much, we risk an overwhelming sense of loss as they face tribu-
lation and death. Weeping is exactly what we are called to do at
times, and the water of our tears can open our souls to accept the
many paradoxes of spiritual life.

Jesus loved to emphasize such ambiguities, as he taught his followers: "Blessed are you who weep now, for you will laugh" (Luke
6:21). He also joined in the tears of others who mourned, as in the
death of his friend Lazarus (John 11:35). Both Mary and Martha
were weeping over their brother Lazarus's death, and both were
angry that Jesus had not been there to stop him from dying, but
Martha (ever assertive) went out to meet Jesus and confront him
about his delay in arriving. The confrontation resulted in Martha's
confession of faith that Jesus is the Messiah, the Child of God
(John 11:27). I can imagine that there was a great deal of weeping
in the household.

Tears express our disappointment in the gap between the way things are and the way we want them to be. Tears manifest the physical pain of grief. And tears can be a form of capitulation, acknowledging that we have been brought to do something that we never thought would be necessary.

This kind of experience makes us feel weak; it can be quite agonizing if we truly feel compassion for the suffering of others. It would be easier not to care, for then we would be spared the physical and spiritual anguish of being present during their pain. We are tempted to raise our defenses, to distance ourselves, not to let intimacy cause us to be hurt. But if we are passionate in faith, we know the world gives us plenty of good reasons to cry.

I think of my friend Richard, who was stricken with multiple sclerosis in his mid-forties. A high school English teacher for many years, he had earned respect and friendship in his community. He had the ability to recite poetry from memory, which he would share frequently in everyday conversation. He enjoyed life, even after he needed to move to a nursing home when his paralysis became severe and he had to use a wheelchair. He was literally unable to roll over in bed, but his mind and spirit and gentle intelligence were fully engaged. Richard shared stories of his accomplishments in teaching, his love for his wife and family, and often asked me to pray with him. Despite the indignities brought about by the multiple sclerosis, Richard held on as long as he could to the identity he had before the onset of his disease. When he died, I was honored to have a part in his memorial service, and I recalled then that Richard's favorite holiday had been Thanksgiving. He was a pilgrim in a barren land in his own way, and I wept with gratitude that I had known him.

Good and evil can *both* be results of suffering. Building a fortress to protect our hearts from pain will also keep us from experiencing the richness of love. In a continuing education seminar on establishing and maintaining professional boundaries, the psychiatrist leading the session explained that appropriate boundaries will allow good things to reach us and keep bad things "outside our bounds." If boundaries are too rigid, we are protected from harm, but also miss out on many opportunities for positive nurture. If boundaries are too relaxed, we can receive love, but are more vulnerable to abuse. Life is a constant process of learning how open and vulnerable we can be, and in what contexts we can allow this to happen. Serving God's children in ministry can open up the most wonderful relationships that can be realized on this earth, even when we are surrounded by so many circumstances we know to be wrong.

≋ Counting the Cost

We make various choices about how to cope with the downside of servanthood, the battered heart. First, we may enter into the experience and probe it more thoroughly. The German poet Rainer Maria Rilke described this as "living the questions." Second, we may decide to avoid the hard questions and select a theological view that answers everything for us. Third, we may pursue our own goals and not attempt to resolve moral and spiritual dilemmas.

The most demanding choice among these three options is the first: to engage theological questions more deeply and to arrive at new understandings of the human condition and our place in God's world. This choice requires commitment, discipline, education, reflection, and help from others. Several biblical texts suggest that God tries our hearts as a test of faith. One person who was mightily tested by God was David, whose life story from childhood to old age is fortunately recorded for us in the books of the Hebrew Scriptures. When David was preparing to step down from the throne so that his son Solomon could assume the duties of kingship, he offered a prayer of farewell. He was celebrating the freewill offering of the people for the construction of the house of Sovereign God: "I know, my God, that you *search the heart,* and take pleasure in uprightness; in the uprightness of my heart I have freely offered all these things, and now I have seen your people, who are present here, offering freely and joyously to you" (1 Chron. 29:17, emphasis added).

These words, spoken in the context of David's intimate and not always obedient relationship with God, showed spiritual maturity. David in later life understood the wrenching experiences of earlier years—battles, death threats, and adultery, among others—as a means whereby God searched his heart and found it not wanting but ripening. David's suffering was not a test coldly conducted, nor was it a pointless punishment. He came to understand his mistakes and accepted the consequences of his actions, and he was able to give thanks to the God who guided him through it all. I like the image of slow growth and ripening as a metaphor for the action of the Holy Spirit in our lives. Rilke has a lovely poem on this theme that carries the original German title, *Ich Liebe dich, du sanftestes Gesetz:*

> I love you, gentlest of Ways,
> who ripened us as we wrestled with you.
>
> You, the great homesickness we could never shake off,
> you, the forest that always surrounded us,
>
> you, the song we sang in every silence,
> your dark net threading through us,
>
> on the day you made us you created yourself,
> and we grew sturdy in your sunlight. . . .
>
> Let your hand rest on the rim of Heaven now
> and mutely bear the darkness we bring over you.[1]

The wrestling and searching, occurring in daylight and darkness, happen on their own quite naturally in the work of justice, peace,

and mercy. But an important corollary to our service itself is
immersion in the knowledge and love of God. When we join
together to worship God, to reflect on God's actions and the history of God's people, we seek God's reality in the midst of our reality. Worship is not simply a source of support, shoring up our good
efforts, but a means of seeking *truth,* seeking to *see the world with
God's eyes.* This causes us to question our own achievements: not
to do away with them, but to improve them. We need to be part of
a worshiping community, among people who will walk with us as
God tests our hearts.

A second option is to ignore the hard questions and operate on a
level where we are comfortable. We may practice avoidance, allowing the final answers to be a mystery, and leave it up to God to
solve. This choice often involves shutting ourselves down emotionally, which is both a personal loss and a loss to those we serve. Poet
Geoffrey Hill describes a soul who tries to keep God out in such a
way, like Donne using the image of God as an entreatant at the
door, bidding entry. Hill's character wonders why God keeps coming back:

> *Lachrimae Amantis*
> What is there in my heart that you should sue
> so fiercely for its love? What kind of care
> brings you as though a stranger to my door
> through the long night and in the icy dew
> seeking the heart that will not harbour you,
> that keeps itself religiously secure?
> At this dark solstice filled with frost and fire
> your passion's ancient wounds must bleed anew.[2]

If God is so persistent, can it be that our rejection of God's challenge leads God to feel pain? Many of us may find that it is easy to
harbor God in our souls for a time, as long as God does not make
too many demands or cause us to feel discomfort or jeopardize our
position in society. Here I think of Peter's rejection of Christ just

before the crucifixion. When Peter failed to acknowledge his relationship with Jesus—denying Christ three times in one night—he realized he had poisoned his own soul (Luke 22:54–62). A similar fear may lead some of us from direct contact with and care for people into safer, more distant roles. In these roles there is less personal tugging at the heart, a more manageable sense of accomplishment. Being sheltered in this way may be tenable for a time, and even desirable for someone who has been wounded by direct service. But we must remain in some way existentially aware of the souls of those in our care. As Christians, we must love our work and the people we serve. Unfortunately, the temptation is to spiritually close the door on those who are served and thus to lose a sense of mission and perspective on the work to which we are called.

Others may seek out a theology that has all the answers, that leaves no room for doubt or question. Some find security in having a firm answer for every concern. Others seek solace in an otherworldly spirituality that does not demand transformation of the current reality, but instead focuses on the vertical relationship with God or the next life. Others blend traditions according to their own preferences, looking for the mixture that seems to conform to their present circumstances rather than conforming themselves and their souls to an ongoing, historical faith. Many believers today have adopted a consumer orientation to spirituality, maintaining that you can "shop around" and compare religions like products in a store. Which brand meets your needs and matches your lifestyle? The hard questions and complex answers can be left on the shelf.

Some Christians try to resolve the ambiguities of sickness by putting primary responsibility on believers. If they only prayed hard enough and long enough, everything would be all right. If something is wrong, it's not God's fault; it's theirs. This very message was preached to a young woman born with a cleft palate. As a teenager, her appearance was far from the standard of conventional beauty. When she attended an evangelical healing service, one person enthusiastically offered to pray for her healing from the condition. She insisted, however, that she had already been healed. She had been blessed by the support of her own congregation, which allowed her to accept herself as beautiful even with a cleft palate. She was able to accept that healing is not the same as curing, that miracles do not always bring outward change.

One of the strengths of the United Church of Christ (UCC) as a denomination is that our theology does not lead members to easy answers. It allows for openness, questioning, and ambiguity, which some would say means the United Church of Christ stands for nothing. On the contrary, I believe the church is the church when it stands for "courage in the struggle for justice and peace," without preordaining the final answers and outcomes. The United Church of Christ historically has been firmly committed to diakonal service and higher education, both areas of life that cause Christians to explore questions deeply rather than accept pat answers.

A third alternative is to focus on our personal ambitions and play the system well enough to get material rewards and still convince ourselves we are serving humanity. This is often a condition of someone whose cynicism has gone unaddressed, who is not subject to the discipline and support of a loving community, who is so effective and successful that people don't want to ask probing questions about the spiritual condition. Arguably, many people in this position are furthering the aims of the church and enabling others to serve quite faithfully. But I wonder about the personal cost paid by anyone who is willing to forgo spiritual wholeness to achieve pragmatic goals while still upholding it as a value within the institution or community. It seems to me that these folks are often a "flash in the pan" who have little staying power. There are many recent examples of profiteering executives in health care who quickly disappeared from the scene when their fraud was exposed. Their selfish and shortsighted behavior has destroyed the heart and soul of many formerly benevolent institutions and ruined the trust of the public in the professions, such as medicine, which had been held in high regard.

Servanthood *should* propel us to question our beliefs, our assumptions, our abilities, and the way the world works. My heart and soul should not be so well defended that I lose the ability to be compassionate or to confess my vulnerabilities. Yet that is the temptation in the role of servant ministry—to have all the answers, to have our act together, to be paragons. Maybe we have given so much energy to defining ourselves in our roles that we have lost touch with who we are as humble souls. We are neither helpless nor all-powerful in the face of the problems we seek to solve. If we are faithful servants, we will accomplish some good things, make some critical mistakes, change our minds, and change our plans. Our goal is not a heart that is invulnerable, but a heart that becomes more knowing and mature as experience lands its inevitable blows upon us. As my husband often reminds me, the best I can hope for in this life is to become a great soul. Here is what it will take.

≋ Four Principles for Seeking Spiritual Integrity

Finding New Definitions of Worth

For one thing, spirituality demands so much *unlearning*. It takes work to unlearn what we have been taught about ego, success, strength, leadership, and power. It takes work to grasp onto definitions taught to us by our parents, our schools, our society, and even some of our churches, and then hold them to the fire of lived experience. For those of us in the developed world, worth equals affluence, high social status, the ability to have power over others, and physical comfort. Spirituality, on the other hand, does not find worth in any of these things; they are irrelevant. We gain worth in spiritual terms through dependence upon God, humility, service to others, and the ability to give thanks.

A colleague described the years he had spent as a pastor in two affluent congregations. There were no rough edges, no harsh realities to disrupt the idyllic conditions established by favorable climate, wealth, and a life of ease. This world was one that secular culture would define as the paradigm of success: to enjoy the fruits of privilege, to indulge in what is most pleasurable. Many of his church members were retired, and their foremost existential question was, How do I lower my golf handicap? This pastor and his family enjoyed their palatial parsonage in this seeming paradise, and surely they were providing ministry in the name of Christ. But this pastor also realized how easy it would be to fall asleep spiritually in such a place.

When we choose a life of Christian service, we are compelled to unlearn cultural definitions that have no lasting value. At the end of the day, do the promises made to us and by us still have integrity? Have we compromised our ethical standards for the sake of our mission? We are constantly confronted by situations that call our commitment into question: Are we willing to take an unpopular position? Will we, just this once, fudge the numbers in the report to make our program look better? Can we follow through on a promise to our children even when work demands arise? Are we justified in lashing out at someone who is making life difficult for us? Answering these questions requires us to spend significant time in prayer and spiritual reflection, alone and with others. We may engage in this reflection while we are writing, painting, exercising, listening to music, raking leaves, or kneading bread. But we all need ways we can open our souls to God and let experiences of pain and pleasure sift through us. It is tempting not to do this work and instead to be satisfied with sentimentality, platitudes, and moralism. We will meet our obligations and cling to whatever satisfaction can be derived from material comforts. But the soul cries out, and God batters our hearts yet again, and we know we must continue the unlearning process so that we will be ready for new learnings.

Living "In but Not of" the System

Another temptation that stands in our way as spiritual seekers is the system within which we serve as diakonal ministers. The much-maligned institutional church, the contemporary world of health and human service ministries, the mindless corporation, the stubborn or unwilling board—any of the structures that must be put in place for a sustained ministry to exist—all of these can draw our attention away from a primary focus on Christ. Maintaining the institution is, of course, necessary and in many ways salutary. We must know the rules to be effective. Mission-driven organizations that are also efficiently run are undoubtedly gifts of God to the wider world. But there is always a danger that the "translation" from faith to function will fall short. Pragmatic concerns demand our attention in a way that spiritual concerns do not. Even when we try to hold the two side by side, it will always be easier to allow prayer and devotions to slip to the bottom of the agenda. If spiritual practices become "optional" in group consciousness, they can easily disappear.

In addition, the politics of church and institutional life can easily consume our energies. I have found myself engaging in lengthy discussions with others about the church, only to realize later that we did not address even tangentially the tenets of faith or core issues of ministry and mission. Instead, our discussions about "the church" were really about personal ambitions, pastoral performance, money, programs, divisions in the congregation, and power. While we seemed to be talking about Christianity, we were talking "around" it. The danger is that we will talk about what surrounds faith and not ever get to the core of what is happening at the deepest level of our souls or the souls of our organizations. Institutional survival requires a canny knowledge of the political game. Saying prayers won't quite solve our problems, keep the doors open, or meet payroll. Or so it seems, until we consider what would happen if we *stopped* praying.

All of us know it is a long way from Jesus' powerful, earthy encounters with persons who came to him for healing to the world in which we function today. The focus for us is treatment, not healing; it is providing services, not serving. It is the organizational structure, not the personal encounter. Our churches are measured by membership rolls, square footage, and charitable giving when the annual reports get written. Fervent prayers and passionate dedication, because they are not quantifiable, go unnoticed by the system.

We know the system well, for we are its caretakers. This world encompasses not only our own complex institutions, but also the many systems within which we operate. We are inundated by information, overwhelmed by initiatives, and forced to speak in a language that will make sense to persons outside the church. It seems there is more than enough talk, and none of it creates needed change. Even caregiving is threatened by bureaucratic regulation and managed care requirements in some settings, as pastoral care staff, for instance, are challenged to prove their value in health care systems. Chaplains collect data from scientific research on the nature and effects of prayer, hoping that they can shore up their positions as a valuable part of the healing team. We operate within the bounds of these systems to our advantage and to our peril, for with every gain comes a corresponding debt. Our obligations are many. They restrain us from exercising charity. They may prevent us from speaking the truth and doing justice. And then we wonder why it seems our mission is lost in the maze as we wander, seeking to find the God who is so elusive in this world.

Yet without institutions, we have no tradition and no stability. The good news is that it is possible to serve God's people even in an organization that is far from perfect as long as we remember that the Spirit is not present merely as window dressing for the institution. Prayers and rituals cannot be just decorations or enhancements to dress up a fundamentally misguided effort. They are the heart of the body. The same is true for our lives. We live for more than ourselves. We live to bring God's dominion more fully to earth, in our own stumbling, halting way. There are signs of hope, as even the entrenched systems of denominationalism continue to move closer together through ecumenical dialogue toward common recognition of sacraments and forms of ministry. As long as there is room for change in a system, there is room for the Holy Spirit to move and to bring redemption.

Understanding Growth as a Means, Not an End

Before we are capable of unlearning the conventional definition of growth, we tend to define it in terms of numbers. Growth is a remarkable panacea to those who wonder whether they are carrying out their mission: "Look, we are growing! We are serving more people! Our budget is bigger! Our buildings are multiplying! Look at the good we are doing." And indeed, Jesus did say, "Thus you will know them by their fruits" (Matt. 7:20). But growth is not necessarily a worthy end in itself, and it may be yet another temptation to abandon spirituality.

We are seduced by size, by scope, by the power and influence they bring. We want people to sit up and take notice of us, to see how well we are doing, how successful we are in carrying out God's work. Some of our religiously affiliated health care providers experience, I believe, a secret gratification that their budgets and staffs are so large in contrast with those of the churches and even denominational instrumentalities. "Why, you could buy and sell us," the church executives say. And our pride swells and we are glad they realize that about us, even though it also puts up a barrier that threatens our ability to relate to the church that gave us birth. The megachurch is a recent trend that gives rise to pride and envy in the world of congregational life. Spacious parking lots become the measure of success. As we utilize marketing and management tools for the sake of Christ's service, we must be careful not to lose sight of our fundamental commitments to the gospel. Bigger is not always better. The product that everyone will buy is not always what is best for everyone.

Our spirits and our minds need to be challenged when we seek shelter in this fallacy. Growth for growth's sake is a secular, not a sacred, value. It exemplifies the way in which we can lose our own language as the church. We adopt catchphrases from the bestseller lists or popular management theory in order to make the gospel relevant and understandable. Leaders of religiously affiliated institutions often talk about "market share," "focus groups," and "stakeholders." The language of the church puts people to sleep and seems archaic, we believe. Federal funding does not allow it (in certain circumstances, that is true). It is not necessary to abandon the language of secular culture. Yet if we completely sacrifice all religious language, we lose one of the key elements of growth—the sense of mission, community, and spirit that can join people together in a common task. If we abandon our individual stories and our faith heritage, we lose an essential reference point and great historical richness.

The story of how my organization developed through the support of nineteenth-century German immigrants in Illinois always inspires me when I pause to examine the mission and purpose of our work. Lifelink was originally founded in 1895, when we opened the doors of the original "Castle" building to a handful of orphaned children and older adults who needed a home and someone to care for them. As a mission of the church, old and young were supported by congregations for miles around through generous offerings and donations of bushels of corn, canned tomatoes, horses, cows, and chickens. Fall festivals drew hundreds of families who gathered on the picnic grounds and even sat on tree branches to listen to long sermons and sing hymns. Churchwomen peeled potatoes for a day and a half, their children running around their ankles, to prepare enough to feed the crowds. Today, the people we serve are more numerous and have more diverse needs, and our volunteers no longer peel potatoes. Yet the dedication and spirit of those early volunteers can hardly be outmatched. Our growth over the century is laudable if it translates into greater, more faithful diakonal ministry. However, if we have achieved only numeric growth without a spiritual foundation, then we have not fulfilled our mission.

Preserving the Language of Faith

Doing good works seems to be one way to maintain the essential spirit of our faith, and I suspect many of us have chosen the path of servant ministry as a way of living out our commitment to the gospel. But what does it mean now that persons with humanistic or nonreligious motives do work in the world that is quite similar to our own? Many of our institutions established for Christian service now blend in with the broader culture. How do we maintain our differentness? The hymn says, "They will know we are Christians by our love." But will our colleagues and the recipients of our care know the difference between our work and that of others? I would argue that an ongoing commitment to spiritual deepening and integrity will have a very subtle and yet profound effect upon our work. The end result of pursuing a more spiritual life is not that we will be known as saints or heroes of faith, but that we might have sufficient strength to continue carrying out our ministry in Christ's name.

Part of this commitment must be embodied in the symbols and the words we use. It seems only preachers and teachers feel the responsibility to preserve the language and powerful imagery of faith in today's world. I have heard discussions by boards of directors intent on raising corporate gifts who feel they should take "Christ" out of the mission statement. A more secular, humanitarian approach seems appropriate for today's business environment. Yet to sacrifice the religious language in a mission statement is to sacrifice institutional soul. Without it, who are we? In discussing ways that Christian organizations have developed organizational ethics statements, one staff member from a nonreligious hospital expressed envy: "You [faith-based agencies] have something to rally around, a common heritage to appeal to that gives you an identity. Everyone in your organization can share some of those religious values, even if they are not Christian, even if the workforce and community is very diverse. At our hospital, there is no common spirit that brings us together."

The words of faith have power and force. When we use them, we call forth an emotional response and a historical memory in people that otherwise would not occur. When we ask for healing or blessing "in the name of Jesus," we state clearly that we are not in this work alone. When we offer to pray for or with people, we demonstrate that our commitment to their welfare is more than casual. When we use religious symbols, we draw upon deep meaning and point people in the direction of transcendence. When we use religious stories or religious names in our conversations, we testify that we are part of a larger river of history and experience.

Our daughters attended a church-based child care center for the first several years of their lives until we needed to move them to a center closer to the public school where our older daughter would start kindergarten. I still remember how wonderful it was to walk down the halls with my babies and see the Sunday school bulletin boards, crosses, Bibles, banners, the Ten Commandments posted for children to learn, and to frequently see the pastors and church staff members visiting with the little boys and girls. What an extraordinary message for them that they could grow up in God's house, the same place where they were baptized. They were part of the daily life of the church, getting visits from the seniors who had their weekly meetings in the lounge, watching funerals take place in the sanctuary, and contributing to the mitten tree during Advent (for children in need of warm winter clothes). Now they attend a secular, proprietary child care center. There are teddy bears, dinosaurs, and the alphabet on the walls, but no faith symbols. The only fundraisers are for internal needs of the child care center rather than for others in the community. None of it is objectionable, but the children and I notice what is missing: a lack of spiritual meaning and emphasis, religious images and rituals, a nurturing church environment.

Most of us find ourselves struggling to speak the language of the world and the language of faith at the same time, generally finding it easier to use the former. Sometimes a secular equivalent will hold the same meaning as a religious expression; sometimes there is no substitute. We can call someone a resident, a patient, a customer, or a client; or we can call someone a member of the family of God, a neighbor, a brother, or a sister. We can praise persons for unselfishness, or we can compare them with the good Samaritan. We can appeal for ethical conduct with the standards of our policy and procedure manuals, or we can subscribe to the Golden Rule. We need boldness and sensitivity to know when it is appropriate, rather than manipulative or exploitive, to use faith language, but it is a vital way to breathe spirit into a life of service.

Using religious words in a sensitive and honest way can transform a perfunctory experience into something with lasting meaning. I think of a friend named Donna who was struggling with a difficult relationship. She asked herself the basic question, "What are the two of us doing together?" Donna realized after a moment that her answer was, "I'm on a mission from God." The relationship was entering hard times, but Donna felt confident that there was a spiritual reason for her to stay invested in the other person's life. She truly believed she had a "calling" to work on the relationship, and that belief sustained her. Donna also has a straightforward, spontaneous way of praying. When she is feeling a bit desperate, she looks up to heaven and says, "God, I could use a little help down here!"

Another wonderful example of the simple, unapologetic use of faith language comes from the former president of Princeton Theological Seminary, James I. McCord. During my first year as a student there, I was deeply moved by the way he read Scripture during our chapel services with such force and conviction. Before he would begin reading the lesson, he would look at us directly from the lectern and solemnly demand, "Listen now for the Word of God as it speaks to you." In those few words he captured my attention and made me feel indeed that the Scripture verses were being directly dictated from God to me. It is a practice I have carried into my ministry.

As we serve others in this world, if we use words at all, let us use words of faith. And let us not use them lightly, but with thanksgiving for the power they carry to remind us who we are and to whom we belong.

≋ **2**

Whose Power Is It Anyway?

For you as yet but knock, breathe,
shine, and seek to mend.
—John Donne

Sometimes I wish I knew all the answers to my questions about power. Who wields it? Who is victimized by it? And whose power is it anyway? Let me share three true stories that cause me to confront the limits of our power.

The first is about Helen and her husband, Bill. They are concerned about Bill's mother, who seems to be forgetting a lot. Eventually, they realize she has Alzheimer's disease, and they cannot allow her to live alone. She moves in with them for a while, but even there her wandering and memory loss create hazards for the whole family. After much soul-searching, they admit Bill's mom to a nursing home for her own safety and care. A couple of years pass by, and Helen and Bill get used to visiting Mother in the Alzheimer's unit of the home. Helen volunteers as a clothing mender. Gradually, the nursing home staff notice Helen visits by herself and Bill stays home. Then for a few months no one visits Mom. Soon afterward, Bill comes to the nursing home—to stay. He, too, has Alzheimer's disease. As Helen brings Bill to his room in the nursing home, there are tears in her eyes. Bill lives down the hall from his own mother. They do not recognize each other.

The second story deals with Freddy's parents, who are reported to the state for child abuse. Freddy is one year old, and his arm was broken when his father beat him. Freddy is placed in a foster home. His parents separate; Mom says Freddy's father beat her too. Mom goes through parenting classes and seeks counseling designed for victims of domestic violence. Freddy and his mother love each other, and after two years have passed, the foster care staff feel they can be reunited. Freddy, now three, returns to live with his biological mom. Four months later Freddy is dead. His mother drowned him in the bathtub as she was holding his head underwater trying to teach him not to be afraid of the water. It is later discovered that, without telling the foster care caseworker, the father had moved back into the home. Both parents go to prison.

The third story concerns a church-related mission in a rural community. For decades it served the people who needed food, clothing, counseling, health care, and other services. Then along comes a casino gambling operation with a state license and plenty of money to buy real estate and contribute to the local tax coffers. The casino operators decide to build a huge casino on land right next to the mission. Pretty soon the city is widening the roads to allow people to get to the casino, and the mission's property is squeezed more and more until operating at its location becomes impossible. After a lengthy battle with the casino operators and city officials, the mission is forced to find a new home.

≈ Sources of Spiritual Power

Where *is* the power that leads to justice and righteousness in our work? When these kinds of events take place right in our own front yards, I have to wonder whether we have any claim to power. Why didn't God step in and make sure these events did *not* happen? Why does it seem so often that the person who is most vulnerable is the one who is made to suffer? I have no desire here to explain "why bad things happen to good people." But I do want to make the point that experiences like these cause us to question, on a spiritual level, the nature of God's power and the scope of our power as Christian servants. I could just as easily share stories of remarkable successes I have witnessed among persons who received care. There are many of them. But I feel we must examine the *source* of power in Christian service: where it comes from, how it is expressed, and how it can be used and misused.

Some of the power in our work derives from the experiences of persons in our care: children who have had the sins of previous generations visited upon them; men and women for whom suffering is a constant companion; vulnerable, elderly people who seek healing; communities and populations of people touched by evil and injustice. There is power in them. Jesus asks us to open ourselves to their power, as he did.

There is power in the church. We cherish that link to tradition, to the saints and martyrs, the common folk, the church fathers, the Marys and Marthas, as well as the living faith of those who gather today in Christ's name.

There is power in our institutions. They have a life and holiness of their own. There is unnameable power in their history, in the story behind the bricks and within the cornerstones, beneath the trees that were planted and sanctify the lives given and the gifts sacrificed, the souls that have gone before us. There is power in our schools, homes, and communities.

There is power in our degrees, our training, our certifications, our titles, our professional associations and stamps of approval, our inspections and peer reviews and ratings and favorable publicity.

There is power in the people who work with us in the vocation of service, from the affluent, influential donors to the employees earning minimum wage to the dedicated volunteers.

There is power in all of these, to one extent or another. But finally, it is *spiritual* power about which we must be fundamentally concerned. Only spiritual power can bring God's righteousness and justice to the world. Spiritual power must ultimately be invested in a person—not in a program, a church, an institution, or a tradition. Without the witness of transformed individuals, our programs, churches, institutions, communities, and even traditions have no power.

We must say, "Yes." We must allow God's Spirit to come and to dwell in our bodies. We must allow spirituality to pervade our lives and work. We must ask God to break down our defenses so that God's Spirit can live in us, in the events of our daily lives. There are many forms of spirituality; find the one that is powerful for you. It should be personal, as God's love for each of us is personal. You may find God in silence, in spoken prayer, in music, in nature, in friendship, in Scripture, in worship, in the arts. The ways are many, but the basic principle is to learn the habit of being, not doing. You learn to practice the presence of God so that eventually God infuses the rhythms of everyday life.

Spirituality is not what you save up for church. Spirituality is in the small, ordinary events of life as well as the major cataclysms. It is with you in triumph and tragedy. It is the argument you had at home, the struggle about a decision at work, the morning you took time to watch the sunrise. Character is not proven in the decisions you make in a few life-changing situations, but is built slowly through the small decisions you make every day.

≋ The Power of One Life

One day I was meeting with a staff member who works in a children's home in Chicago. She was describing her duties as a social work supervisor in this institution, caring for children who have a history of sexual violence. At a certain point I was not listening to her anymore, because all I could think about was the way that this young woman was willing to take on seemingly intractable problems, and that her work with these children truly relied on only one thing: her humanity.

When we are serving or caring for others, at the most elemental level our only resource is the soul. If somehow we have developed enough character, enough guts, enough insight within ourselves, this fragile essence of soul is the bottom line. This is all we have to offer. And what a beautiful thing it is that God has put that healing essence inside us. Servanthood is all about learning to bring it out, to share it more and more fully. And the more a soul is devoted to service, the more powerful it becomes, as Peg Thompson describes in *Finding Your Own Spiritual Path:*

> Truly compassionate service—whether we are giver or receiver—happens when we are moved by the sacred within and around us. It is not so much something we do or receive but something we are blessed with. We recognize that we are taking part in a sacred cycle of caring and healing, simultaneously giving and being given to, helping and being helped, caring and being cared for, healing and being made whole. . . . If we are straining to be compassionate because we think we should be, it is not real caring. Our compassion grows out of our listening for the subtle complexities of events.[1]

We can access the power of the soul through physical touch. Those of us who work in health care have a special gift in that we care quite literally for persons' bodies. Our spirituality can never stray too far from the real world of God's people, it can never be carried into irrelevancy or overintellectualizing, because we must always come back the next day and face the minutiae of bodily needs and human limits. The needs that surround us, often considered our enemy, can also be a spiritual teacher.

Jesus gives us power. I continue to be amazed by the force of his words to the disciples as recorded in John 15. The story takes place during the Last Supper, and we are told that after dinner was served, Jesus took up a towel and performed the work of a servant as he washed the disciples' feet. He then told them,

> I do not call you servants any longer, because the servant does not know what the master is doing; but I have called you friends, because I have made known to you everything that I have heard from my Parent. You did not choose me but I chose you. And I appointed you to go and bear fruit, fruit that will

last, so that the Parent will give you whatever you ask the Parent in my name. I am giving you these commands so that you may love one another. (John 15:15–17)

Thus, we are friends of the Messiah, friends of Jesus Christ, not just well-intentioned do-gooders. On the basis of this friendship we carry out our work of service, bearing fruit in his name.

≋ The Power of Humility

An equally profound spiritual lesson relates to our lack of power. There are times when we become very comfortable and begin to feel quite satisfied with ourselves and easily forget who has given us the commission, the gifts, and the calling for our work. There is a strong temptation even in a life of servanthood to glorify the self, to pile up titles and degrees, to expand our holdings and our budgets as a means of demonstrating our worth to the wider world. When our ministries succeed, they can take on a new power of their own and may too readily depart from their original mission. The power of faithful leadership begins to be seen as an anachronism, and we are frustrated to be perceived as serving in a "backwater," as existing on the margins of mainstream culture.

Everywhere glory is awarded to individual success and affluence, and there are few rewards for plodding, patient participation in Christian community and the formation of servant leadership. This is particularly true for parents and for retired persons. The world does not always value people whose work is quiet and without a title, and I often witness a condescending attitude toward those who see "home" as a significant place for service.

We may begin to feel that we deserve a lot of credit for the self-sacrificing work we have done. We may feel entitled to recognition and status for our acts of servanthood. At these times we can turn to a very old story in Deuteronomy 8:1–20, in which Moses warned the Israelites against the eternal temptations of pride and self-sufficiency. After surviving their forty-year journey through the wilderness, the people were looking forward to enjoying life in Canaan, and Moses had to make them aware of the perils of prosperity. People will forget God and believe that their affluence is the result of human power and efforts alone. Remember how God humbled and tested us like a loving parent, Moses said.

> Take care that you do not forget the Sovereign God, by failing to keep divine commandments, ordinances, and statutes, which I am commanding you today. . . . Do not say to yourself, "My power and the might of my own hand have gotten me this wealth." But remember the Sovereign God, for it is God who gives you power to get wealth, so that God may confirm the divine covenant that God swore to your ancestors, as God is doing today. (Deut. 8:11, 17–18)

We are more directly confronted by our lack of power when our work does not produce the results we anticipated. There are many historical examples of faith-inspired groups who have gone forth to do good work in Christ's name and have found they had little effect. Nineteenth-century diakonal workers in Germany began to assume responsibility for many social problems, with limited success. Naturally, the lack of obvious change troubled them: "Even though communities began to take matters into their own hands, the earth did not become a paradise. . . . Programmes and ideals, however, were not enough to wipe poverty off the face of the earth."[2]

Then, if we listen to the spirituality of the Gospels, we recall that we are not in this service to achieve a specific outcome. Religious life has value even when it does not lead to material changes. Reinhold Niebuhr states this well:

> Jesus did not counsel his disciples to forgive seventy times seven in order that they might convert their enemies or make them more favorably disposed. He counselled it as an effort to

approximate complete moral perfection, the perfection of God. He did not ask his followers to go the second mile in the hope that those who had impressed them into service would relent and give them freedom. He did not say that the enemy ought to be loved so that he would cease to be the enemy. He did not dwell upon the social consequences of these moral actions, because he viewed them from an inner and a transcendent perspective.[3]

Courage and radical trust are essential to allow ourselves to be open to the powerful lessons of servant ministry. Comfort, when it comes, derives only from God to us. The Heidelberg Catechism of 1563 adopted by the German Reformed Church, one of the predecessor bodies of the United Church of Christ, describes God as primarily the One who comforts us. In fact, the Latin root of the word "comfort" means "with courage." In those moments when it seems our service is in vain, God is with us to say, "Well done, good and faithful servant." We then have the strength to begin again.

Sometimes not getting the results we wanted protects us from the common danger of assuming too much power in our spiritual lives. In his 1984 book *The Politics of Spirituality,* William Stringfellow emphasizes that biblical spirituality involves "the renunciation of worldly power and the condiments that commonly are associated with worldly power: wealth or the control thereof, success, fame, applause, ambition, avarice, goals, competitive esprit, and the rest of the success syndrome."[4] These are the incentives Satan offered to Jesus in the wilderness, the very types of power Jesus absolutely refused (Luke 4:6). The same temptations are tantalizingly held out to us today even in the world of Christian service. The lures of money and influence are difficult to resist in favor of the quiet accomplishments of a growing faith.

Stringfellow echoes the theme I noted in the introduction to this book. Christian spirituality will not necessarily lead to success in a worldly sense, and it may drive us in the opposite direction. Jesus warns his followers in John 15:18: "If the world hates you, be aware that it hated me before it hated you." We must be careful even as we engage in spiritual exercises that we do not believe they will earn us justification, which is given by the discretion of God. The Spirit calls us to surrender attempts to justify ourselves, to manipulate others, or insist on particular outcomes because we can live by trust. Christian life is indeed a narrow path.

≈ The Power of God

Whose power is it anyway? It is always God's power, and spirituality is our way of appreciating this divine vision. As we participate in this sacred power, we become whole, knowing we are not the owners or wielders of the power, but those who can see it and point others in its direction. When we are spiritually aware, life itself becomes a form of giving thanks to God for all that is. Stringfellow says, "Whatever we do is transfigured into a sacrament of that praise."[5]

The spiritual power and mystery of Christian service are not a one-way transfer. As instruments of Christ's healing power, we find Jesus becomes more present to us in the act of serving. In the work we do, we do not give away our power and we do not condescend to care for the less fortunate—we find the power of God. We are not better or more powerful than the people we care for, as Frederick Herzog notes in a chapter on the development of diakonal ministry in Germany and the United States:

> Primarily the poor and sick does not need me, but I need him. Is it not in the poor and sick that I meet Christ and in this encounter learn to love with the love of God? Is it not in the lowliness of the outcast that I am confronted with God's very being? Christ? The love of God? God's very being? In the poor and the sick? In the outcast?[6]

This is the crucial difference between service offered in Christ's name and service provided for secular or humanitarian reasons. The power that emanates from spiritually inspired efforts points as a witness to the power of God. Those who serve others do not have power in themselves. It can only come to them from God through the act of serving. The power of God fueling our individual and corporate efforts in diakonal ministry is stronger and more sustaining than any purely human motive.

We cannot forget the vital link between spirituality and religious service, for to do so is to diminish God. Rabbi Abraham Heschel lamented in the 1960s that the great religions of the world, which primarily point toward the divine mystery, had become nothing but big social service agencies. Our faith can do so much more, as long as we allow God to direct our wills, grant us visions, and dwell within our souls.

≋ Finding and Renewing Our Power

There are five ways to find the locus of power and renewal that lies at the heart of our work.

History and the Test of Experience

One of the blessings of the spiritual life is that its teachings have not changed significantly over the centuries of recorded history. If we found a manuscript of scientific or mathematical principles written before the time of Christ, it would clearly be outdated and modern knowledge would supersede it. Yet any of us can turn to the Psalms (such as Pss. 8; 23; 31; 100; 121; 139) and find expressed in these eloquent verses many of the same spiritual concerns and hopes we feel today. There is spiritual power in these voices from the past—not only in Scripture but also in devotional writings from Christians such as Julian of Norwich, Martin Luther, Dietrich Bonhoeffer, and Dorothy Day, to name only a few.

Finding these spiritual classics is easier today thanks to wider availability of communication technology. *Devotional Classics* is a good collection of selected readings, and you may sample some of them and see whether their ideas and reflections match the test of your experience.[7] When I turn to such writers, it is for motivation, inspiration, and the sense that someone out there thinks I am on the right track. I hope they will provide you with new energy and power for your life of service.

Prayer

Because prayer is such a common experience, because it is so easy to do and requires no money or equipment, I think we often underestimate its power. We make joking references about prayer being our last resort, and in desperate situations even say someone "hasn't got a prayer." I can think of few things more powerful than prayer in spiritual life.

Some recent scientific studies have recorded the remarkable effects of prayer. Thought-provoking authors have written volumes about ways to pray and types of prayer. Prayer is a vital part of any Christian liturgy. Prayer is revered by every type of Christian church, across the spectrum from conservative to liberal.

What I would like to emphasize here is the power of prayer upon the life of the person who is praying. Prayer is a way of opening the door that usually stands closed between God and each of us. Eugene Peterson describes prayer in this way: "We pray out of conviction that the genius of being human is the ability to be in communion with God. As that communion matures it gathers every detail of our lives—body, spirit, environment, relationships—into a God-animated aliveness, which is spirituality."[8]

When we use prayer as much to listen as to talk, it is the most significant way we can hear God "knock, breathe, shine, and seek to mend." Romans 8:26 tells us that the Spirit helps us to pray when we do not know what to say. Prayer reminds us that we are the petitioners, not the source of power. Prayer is the only way we can confess our sins and beg for liberation from the crushing weight of guilt. Prayer is something we can do before we begin a task and when we have done all that can be done. Prayer gives us incredible power to make a difference in the lives of individuals and communities. Prayer is one way we can express our love for God and for other people. Prayer is a mystery that we can explore and participate in every day that we are alive. Prayer shapes and changes us from the inside out. Prayer is an ancient, primal force in human life that is both timeless and urgent. Prayer has no limits, and it removes our limits. When we pray, we touch God's power and God's power dwells in us.

Spiritual Passion

We discover our power when we tap into our passions. Spiritual life deepens our experience of both love and anger. I use anger as the corollary to love because I believe that in spiritual life, anger is more prevalent than hatred. Jesus told us not to hate our enemies, and he demonstrated that lesson throughout his life. Hatred takes away the humanity of our enemies, making their sin irredeemable, eradicating the possibility of reconciliation. At the same time, hatred makes our enemies more important than they should be—in a way, it deifies them in a negative way and takes away a disproportionate amount of our energy and attention. Hatred, like love, can be a long-term commitment.

However, Jesus did openly express anger. On two occasions, only a day apart, Matthew's Gospel (21:12–19) records that Jesus cursed a fig tree because it did not have any fruit when he was hungry (a seemingly petty flare of anger) and Jesus cleansed the Temple of merchants who had made it a marketplace (an understandable expression of outrage). And in Ephesians 4:26 we read: "Be angry but do not sin; do not allow the sun to go down on your anger." Anger does not have the same staying power as hatred, and though it, too, can be a destructive force, it also has the power to expose what is wrong and what needs to be changed.

When we are free enough to open ourselves up to the habits of spiritual discipline, we find that love emerges as from a deep well and occasionally breaks to the surface of our lives in overwhelming and unexpected ways. My spiritual development is quite small compared with that of others. Nonetheless, since I have devoted more time to spirituality, I find I feel much greater empathy and a sense of connection to people's experiences. This is terrifying sometimes, such as when I feel deeply sad about a tragedy that occurred to someone I only read about in the newspaper. It is wonderful at other times, such as when I feel a joyful love bubbling up while I get together with young children or older adults. Tears of joy and pain spring to my eyes more easily than they did before, and sometimes I have experiences of insight or compassion when I am with another person that are so strong I can actually feel the knowledge on a physical level and a spiritual level.

Spiritual passion can lead us to love people we would never choose to love or even care about; it makes us more vulnerable and less vulnerable at the same time; it makes our lives incredibly full of wonder and yet painfully sensitive to injustice. Spiritual passion can lead to a quickly developing sense of anger, the anger of righteous indignation. For the more we love, the more we cannot tolerate abuse, the cheapening of human life, corruption of power, and all of the forces that hold us back from fully embracing the abundant life God wants for us. Like Jesus, we can use our anger at injustice to fuel efforts for reform.

Powerful experiences of both love and anger—spiritual passion—are signs that we are spiritually alive. They are emotions we would like to put off to another time, or not to feel at all. The shadow side of healing love and righteous anger is self-righteousness, an attitude that feels so well deserved that it is sometimes hard to resist. As we struggle with these unwanted emotions, we are reminded of the importance of confessing our sins and praying for a new and right spirit. But this is an inevitable outcome of soulful living. It is the life to which God calls us.

Grief and Death

A group of sailors were stranded in lifeboats during World War I. It took several days for rescuers to find them, and before they arrived, some of the men had died. Strangely enough, the first to die from privations at sea were the younger sailors. Doctors later decided that the older sailors survived because they had been through more crises over the years and knew that life could go on.

Grief and death teach us this same powerful lesson. When we are able to come face-to-face with mortality, we realize we are all in the same lifeboat. Some of us are cursing our fate and watching for sharks; others are giving thanks to God for saving us and are enjoying every moment of life we are given.

Death shows us that worldly power can be taken away in an instant, and that the money, possessions, and roles we so carefully guard and protect will disappear. After my years of ministry with older adults, I have learned two things: relish good health as long as it is given to you and never take it for granted; and spiritual life is the one thing no one can ever take away from you. You may lose your loved ones, your freedom, your health, your savings, your home, your job, and even your reputation. But no force on earth can steal your soul—your spiritual life remains with you from birth to old age, no matter how your physical circumstances might change. There is much power in that knowledge, and it is a lesson only grief and death can teach us.

Forgiveness

I have saved forgiveness for last because it seems to me that no power in the world has more damaging consequences than resentment and regret and no power is more liberating and life-affirming than forgiveness. Lingering guilt feelings are toxins in our spiritual lives. Lack of repentance and forgiveness can lead to a living death for some people, which is worse for some people than actual bodily death. Painful conflicts from our past dwell with us as the dark side of memory. On the other hand, when we can achieve reconciliation and begin again after an injury or rift in a relationship, we are blessed with a resurrection to new life. Forgiveness is a form of spiritual healing that is as miraculous as any physical healing.

Many years ago, I knew a woman named Myrtle who had advanced Parkinson's disease. It had caused her slowly to become paralyzed, until she could hardly move. With help, she could still eat and talk. Myrtle was one of the members of my Bible study group, but she rarely shared much information about herself. The paralysis had even made it difficult for Myrtle to show emotion. One day, to my surprise, she asked me to visit her in her room at the nursing home. When I entered, she asked me to close the door. Then she asked me, twice, if we were alone in the room. Yes, I assured her. Lying on her bed, she began to cry. Practically whispering, she asked, "What does it take to get into heaven?" I answered that we must believe in God, ask to be forgiven of our sins, and accept Christ fully into our lives.

There was a long pause. Then Myrtle said, "I once hurt my mother. Very badly." I asked her if it was a physical injury. She said yes. Very slowly she shared a bit of her story, that she had been single all her life, that she had been an alcoholic, and that her mother had come to live with her in her elder years. Myrtle said it was during that time she had hurt her mother. "I'm so sorry. But I never told anyone. I'm so ashamed." We spent a long time talking and being silent together and then prayed. It was a powerful experience to watch the thick cloud of shame that had built up over two decades come to the surface and be burned away by the light of God's forgiveness. I wondered whether Myrtle's guilt had caused her to be spiritually immobilized just as the Parkinson's caused her physical paralysis.

We underestimate the healing power of forgiveness. Unaware of its power, we hoard our injuries and build walls around our pain. In so doing, we imprison ourselves as well as those whom we refuse to forgive. Spiritual life whispers to us of the prospect of freedom. Let us open our hearts to hear it.

≋ 3

Entry Points and
Ultimate Meaning

That I may rise, and stand.
—*John Donne*

≋ Motivation: Found and Lost

Why are we called to ministry in institutions of the church? Many
of us would say it is because Jesus said this is what we should do,
because our love for Christ compels us to reach out with compassion to those in need, because we are angry at life's unfairness, or
because we want to help care for people. Worthy motives all, but
are they enough to sustain us over the long term?

Will these motivations allow us to engage fully our whole selves
in our ministries, or will they cause us to go off balance in the
pathology of self-righteousness or self-abnegation? We all know
people who are so carried away by their lofty goals that others who
do not share their agenda become the objects of derision. Such persons cannot see the irony of their behavior when passionate
Christianity turns into hatred and violence. On the other side are
those who allow their Christian convictions to be buried so deeply
beneath layers of professional expertise that their faith is barely
accessible. I will always remember my first encounter with two vet-
eran hospital chaplains, whose faces seemed smooth masks of non-
expression and whose demeanors were so passive that they seemed
almost absent from the room. I said to them, "Either you have seen
a lot in your ministry, or you have really bad kids!" Fortunately,
they laughed.

Feelings of sympathy or concern for the plight of needy persons are not sufficient in themselves to provide a foundation for a long-term vocation of service to others. They must be accompanied by the structure of religious faith, or we risk that the forces of cynicism and experience will cause them to wither and die, or to become corrupted. Theologian Reinhold Niebuhr addressed this directly in a series of lectures he gave in 1932 on religion and the social worker: "To help those who are in need is an ambition which is prompted by the most natural of all human impulses, sympathy. But only when natural sympathy is reinforced by a religious belief that the ultimate value in life is love, can the emotion of sympathy, which like all emotions is unstable and transient, be made the basis of a vocation."[1]

How often do we encounter people who are in emotionally draining jobs and simply run out of steam? Our motivation becomes worn down by a series of frustrations. Our best intentions seem to go nowhere. We find we do not have the appropriate gifts for the occupation we have chosen. Family needs, friendships, health problems, and financial concerns require our attention. Our emotional and mental health suffers. Churches and organizations change, and we wonder whether we still "fit" in the new scheme of things. We are disappointed, disillusioned, and disenchanted. We complain that we are too busy doing petty tasks instead of what is most important. What has happened to our original sense of God's calling?

A divine calling and the sense that you are doing something important in the world in fact make it *more* likely that you will find your inner resources depleted. If your work is very important to you, you will probably experience what psychologists call burnout at least once or perhaps a number of times. This state is caused by excess demands on your energy and coping mechanisms. Symptoms of burnout include spiritual exhaustion, inability to care about things formerly important to you, loss of judgment, and lack of empathy. Naturally, burnout undermines your ability to serve persons in need. You lose the ability to be self-aware, you lose closeness with others, and you lose a proportional sense of your role in God's work in the world.

Those of us engaged in Christian service know that our most impassioned efforts are but a single drop in the huge waterfall of loving service that is needed in this world. But the nitty-gritty daily routine is still important. We may not change a life every day, we may not change the world, but a simple, supportive gesture may be remembered as a life-saving act. Writing a report, making a phone call, and just showing up so that people know we are there—these are not trivial forms of service, as one of my colleagues reminds me. In pastoral care, sometimes the best gift we can provide is our presence and our commitment to remain present with another person. Yet even these basic forms of caring for others, when practiced with spiritual generosity, will lead to exhaustion at times. When we realize that we have come to this point, we need a time of reflection and reassessment, examining what this experience may be telling us. Meeting with a spiritual director or going on a retreat may restore balance to life. (See chapter 7 for other recommendations.)

Unfortunately, you may choose a less healthy path. It is easy in these stressful situations to lash out, angrily condemning persons who appear to be blocking your progress and causing you to overwork: "I deserve more, I deserve better, and this situation is intolerable. It is up to *them* to change it." In this state you become angry, defensive, resistant, resentful, and no longer open to constructive criticism. It is impossible for you to see clearly.

The opposite extreme is to choose passivity. This is a decision to drag your feet, to refuse to make all of your opinions known, to be carried by the tide of others' actions, to sit and observe. After all, raising objections or making your own changes will ultimately be a tiring and fruitless task. There are many outlets for subtle aggression in this path.

Quitting a job may be the result of either of these choices. We may resign in anger in the former case, or slip out quietly in the latter. In both instances, we allow the spiritual power to remain with the seemingly unjust situation, which is surely not our goal.

Emotions will always be strong, but the Spirit of God should still be recognized and respected in the midst of this decision. Terminating our involvement in a ministry should be a profoundly engaging experience, an extension of the original call to ministry itself. To leave with a spirit of rejection and anger, or to leave without revealing to others the personal cost of the decision, is an alternative that denies what is really at stake. Our attitudes toward conflict, change, and leave-taking reveal our deepest articulation of why we are in ministry and what we hope to accomplish. Sadly, I have often witnessed (in my own life and in others' lives) an assumption that when all is going well, it means that God is with us, and when things turn sour, human failings receive the blame.

It seems from my reading of Scripture that both success and failure can be indications of God's hand at work. Clearly, God's prophets faced much human opposition as they carried out divinely ordained work. In the Hebrew Scriptures we read the story of Ruth and Naomi, both widowed and without hope, who managed to build a new life by supporting each other and remaining faithful to God. In the Christian Scriptures, the apostle Paul persevered through beatings and imprisonment to carry the gospel to the Gentiles who otherwise would never hear of Jesus Christ. Their hardship was not an indication that they were on the wrong track; it was only a part of their journey through this world.

Why is burnout so hard for us in diakonal ministry to diagnose and treat? Often we believe our experience of being called by God makes us special. Ministry is sometimes termed the "highest calling," and there are many comments about people in ministry having priority access to "the Person upstairs," or reporting directly to God. Some people have an unrealistic expectation that Christian servants have a superfaith that is somehow stronger and more resilient than the faith of others. God must have chosen me for a reason, many Christian servants will say. I ought to be exempt from this fatigue. After all, many biblical verses imply that God will provide for those who are faithful, that God will renew the strength of those who labor on God's side, such as this quotation from Isaiah:

But those who wait for God shall renew their strength,
they shall mount up with wings like eagles,
they shall run and not be weary,
they shall walk and not faint. (Isa. 40:31)

≋ A Change in Direction

But a question that has occurred to me is: Are we in this work because we are so good at helping people, or has God put us in this work because we are the ones in need of healing? Perhaps God has brought us to this work as an *invitation* to spirituality, as an opportunity to grow in grace. As we provide service to others that is unquestionably needed, is it perhaps also significant that each of us is challenged to engage in the work of becoming a great soul? In this way, we remember to put the spirit first in our lives, prior to the needs of "our work," whatever that may be. We live as co-creators of God's dominion on earth, which becomes visible as we engage in this work of the soul.

We have a prayer group for staff at Lifelink. It is an informal group, and whoever is able to attend each time simply shares joys and concerns and needs for prayer. Sometimes we are able to let our guard down and trust one another enough to really admit some serious problems. Our prayer list includes a mother who is in the early stages of Alzheimer's disease; a relative enduring a very prolonged, nasty divorce; a woman in her mid-forties with breast cancer; a one-year-old granddaughter who has died; a friend being treated for clinical depression. We are only a handful of the staff—how many problems are there among the other employees? We are the ones who are supposed to be caring for others, and yet we have many concerns of our own. We need to admit to those we serve and lead that the search for wholeness is something we all share. No one has perfectly achieved it. Perhaps many of us in diakonal ministry have chosen this path because we have a particularly strong need to pursue wholeness and healing. Robert K. Greenleaf, in his

book *Servant Leadership*, tells a story of a seminar held for ministers and psychiatrists engaged in healing of the mind and soul. As
the group gathered and began to explore why they had chosen this
profession and what motivated them, they agreed quickly on the
same reason: "For our own healing."[2]

Let me clarify immediately that I do not understand religious
vocation and purpose to be merely a form of self-help or therapy.
Christian service should not be seen primarily as a source of self-
gratification. That would be a serious misuse of God's calling. It is
quite dangerous for persons with significant emotional or spiritual
problems to engage in work that involves use of religious authority.
Impaired judgment by someone in a serving role damages individual lives, damages the reputation of the church, and can potentially
damage the spiritual health of a whole community of people.

However, I do believe God calls individuals into ministry not
because we are perfect but because we have the capacity to listen
and understand. A person who can hear the voice of God in everyday life can be called to Christian service over and over again.
Religious calling is not a one-time event. Vocation is a changing,
dynamic relationship, involving our inner selves and the communities of people we serve. As we periodically reexamine our motive
and our purpose in servanthood, we can see its potential for changing ourselves, not just changing the world. Our sense of motive and
purpose is best sustained by listening for God, who speaks in and
through our experiences.

To me, a servant-leader is someone who can take a rich variety of
life experiences and fold them into the caregiving role. There is not
necessarily any need to edit out humbling experiences or to
overemphasize moments of success. Even the humdrum routine of
daily maintenance tasks can be woven into spiritual life instead of
being seen as a distraction.

As a working mother, I often feel annoyed by the time I must
spend commuting, washing dishes, doing laundry, shopping for
groceries, and taking care of other "nonspiritual" occupations with
very little intrinsic appeal. I resent the time these duties take away

from being with my children or doing something more enjoyable or fulfilling. But a book on meditation with the wonderful title *Wherever You Go, There You Are* gave me the idea to fill these times with prayer. This approach changed my whole routine. Now as I drive to work in the morning, I spend the thirty minutes in silence, either praying to God or thinking about people on my prayer list. When I mop the floor or cook a meal, I think about the ways in which I appreciate my husband and our two daughters. "Homemaker" duties no longer seem like time wasted, but (on good days!) can become time devoted to the people I love. The hymn "O Grant Us, God, a Little Space" captures the way that awareness of God's presence can transform daily work into prayer:

> On daily work you shed your grace, and blessings all
>   around.
> Yours are the workplace, home and mart, the wealth of
>   sea and land;
> The worlds of science and of art are fashioned by your
>   hand.
> Work shall be prayer, if all be wrought as you would
>   have it done;
> And prayer, by you inspired and taught, shall then with
>   work be one.[3]

This spiritual perspective on a life of service calls us to lay down the burden of providing our own motivation and instead allow the Spirit to breathe through our lives and our work. Keeping this truth in mind is often difficult. We are more accustomed to taking credit for ourselves than taking ourselves out of the picture. When we understand diakonal ministry as *our work*, we overestimate our abilities. It is God who does the work, and it is God whom we serve.

There are dangers for both introverts and extroverts in the work of servant ministry. Introverts may find that the constant demands for care and the high level of human need overwhelm any time they might claim for themselves in order to reenergize and renew their spiritual lives. You never come to the end of your work in caregiving, no task is ever complete, there is always a new problem or opportunity around the corner, and what you are ultimately trying to accomplish is intangible. All of this may be devastating to a person who needs considerable solitude and reflection in order to serve most effectively. Claiming that time may seem selfish to some, and unnecessary to others.

Extroverts, on the other hand, may get carried away by the adrenaline surge that comes from being surrounded by a congregation or community that looks to them as a leader. They thrive on the challenge and the human contact, but may feel lonely after a while. Many servant-leaders have few peers in their church or organization and no one to serve as their pastor or spiritual guide. A change in direction will help people in any of these situations whose spiritual gauge is running on empty.

≈ Reexamining Your Call

The wisest choice for anyone in Christian service, regardless of temperament, is to revisit our calling and purpose periodically to see which aspects remain valid and which areas need to be redefined. The early American Congregationalists required that church members present evidence of their conversion. This recalling of stories was so ritualized that they developed several categories to describe types of conversions: gradual, sudden, violent, mild, or scarcely perceptible.[4] Malcolm Warford, in the booklet *Our Several Callings* published by the United Church of Christ, describes our religious calling not as a lightning bolt but as a meandering journey: "Vocation is not a matter of a single, unchanging sense of purpose. The fact is that throughout our lives we live in the midst of several callings, changing times and new understandings of God's voice which calls us."[5]

Warford goes on to describe the vocational struggle of Thomas Merton, a Trappist monk and writer. Merton thought he *ought* to be a monk, when in fact his fundamental, natural vocation was to be a writer. This tension itself became a creative force for him. The conflict was not one Merton would have chosen, but it became part of his identity and formation. Warford also tells the interesting tale of Martin Luther King Jr., whose work as a scholar and pastor was interrupted by the *Brown v. Board of Education* decision by the U.S. Supreme Court, which struck down segregation in schools. As the civil rights movement intensified, King's vocation became one of prophetic leader rather than congregational minister. The change was the result of outward rather than inward events, but is nonetheless instructive in the ways that God redirects us. Warford concludes, "God does not require us to know exactly where we are going. Faithfulness requires a certain flexibility that permits us to change course as the wind blows and shifts direction. God asks us to be ready for those moments, to reach out and to move with the Spirit who leads us to unexpected places and purposes."[6]

≋ Finding New Purpose

Does our life purpose remain the same from youth to old age? Or do we state it that way because it is simpler to grasp? A vocational promise, like any covenantal promise, needs to be reviewed and renewed as we mature and develop in our spiritual lives. We may be pushed into this reexamination when our lives are at a point of ruin, or we can enter into this process from a position of health. Either way, it is good to acknowledge that calling is not static, unchanging, and one-sided. God's call is a lively, dynamic, and challenging dialogue.

Perhaps we limit the concept too much if we identify our sense of vocation with one role (i.e., parent, nurse, teacher, pastor, etc.). When the time comes that we are no longer active in that role for one reason or another, have we lost our sense of calling? No. Vocation cannot be narrowly defined as a certain primary occupation. Instead, vocation is about our identity as Christian disciples. We may be people of faith, but none of us has fully achieved salvation—vocation is a journey and a goal as we "work out" our salvation little by little. In this sense, vocation is never finished. It naturally changes with our life situation and life stage, and in many cases gives shape and meaning to our journey of Christian maturity.

If we turn again to the definition of *diakonia,* which is work that expresses love and compassion, we can see that this spirit can infuse virtually any worthy life path. A group of Lifelink staff gathered for the course "Mission, Vision, and Values," and we asked them, "Does your church recognize the work you do as a form of ministry? If not, would you like that to happen?" This group included nurses, social workers, maintenance staff, food service directors, administrators, support staff, a therapist, and a volunteer director—all very dedicated people. Their response to the question was, "Why should we be singled out? You can do ministry in *any* job. It is the spirit you bring to your work that makes it a ministry. If the church is going to recognize us in some special way, they need to do the same for a lot of people who work in fields other than health and human services."

In this sense, a religious calling *does* last forever, even if a person may work in several occupations over a span of years. Because God's calling to us is to be disciples in whatever we do, we will undoubtedly pursue a variety of occupations and roles in our lives as we experience inner transformation through the life of faith. Ronald Cole-Turner, in another UCC publication titled *Hearing God's Call,* describes this experience: "Probably the most important message is that our calling, as Christians, is not found first of all in our job or career. Our calling is to belong to Jesus Christ. Our calling is to be part of the community of Christ and to join in its mission."[7]

Here, too, our Pilgrim ancestors had studied the life of faith enough to know that there are stages of redemption. They wisely understood that calling is ongoing, and they catalogued it this way: you are humbled; then called; you walk with Christ; you experience weaknesses; you are given special providences; you encounter temptations; and you are finally delivered by God to ultimate redemption.[8]

Sometimes our purpose changes in a positive direction. A minister who became a quadriplegic after neurological surgery went on to work as a chaplain among others who used wheelchairs. A young mother whose preschool-age children attended Head Start during a time when the family's finances were very limited later developed the skills to work as an administrative assistant in the same organization that had helped educate her children. A teenager whose best friend was killed in a drunk-driving accident began to educate high school students about the dangers of drug and alcohol abuse.

However, at other times changes in our sense of purpose and vocation are devastating. In recent years, many members of the clergy have had to face disciplinary review for alleged pastoral misconduct. In these tragic and emotionally charged proceedings, it is difficult enough to establish whether the complaints are justified. If they are, the harder question remains: Is he or she still called by God to ministry? In cases of poor judgment or egregious misconduct, what has happened to the pastor's calling? Is it still valid? The denominational body may choose to answer, "We cannot question God's calling, but we can address the church's affirmation of your call." In some cases, the church can no longer validate the person's appropriateness for authorized ministry. This decision does not necessarily void the pastor's previous faithful service and sense of call.

A similar question arises when people divorce. If the couple was married in a church, the officiant most likely proclaimed during the wedding ceremony, "What God has called together, let no one put asunder." If the covenant ends with a divorce, has God's calling for them to live together as a married couple also ended? If God brought them together, is it God who has called them apart? Ideally, a marriage covenant holds enough breadth to allow for one or both partners to make alterations in their vocational direction or life purpose. Any marriage over the years evolves into a series of marriages, and our commitment and promises change as our life situation changes. But there are some marital relationships—for example, those in which there has been repeated abuse—that wrongfully inhibit the growth and Christian maturity of the marriage partners. In such cases I do believe God calls persons to leave the relationship in order to pursue health and wholeness for the sake of their own souls. However, this decision does not necessarily mean that everything that has gone before was wrongheaded, mistaken, or valueless. Spiritual life reminds us that we cannot alter the past to conform to the needs of the present. Neither should we be limited by the record of history in making our decisions in the current moment. God's grace redeems us and allows us every day to begin life again with *new* purpose.

If we look at the Hebrew Scriptures' book of Jonah, we see that God will at times compel us to take the good news to places we would never choose. Jonah was called to preach to the people of Nineveh, but he tried to escape that assignment by literally sailing away. God was not ready to let Jonah off the hook, instead creating a storm that threw Jonah overboard. While he thrashed about in the sea, Jonah was swallowed by a big fish and spent three days in the fish's belly. Jonah then capitulated and prayed to God from inside the fish. By the time the fish spat him out on the shore, Jonah was ready to go to Nineveh and preach. His preaching convinced the Ninevites to believe in God, who was so impressed by their repentance that God decided not to punish them for their past wickedness. This short book is a classic illustration of the way we resist God's efforts to save us.

Moses' journey of faith also reminds us that God engages in two-way dialogue with us. In the famous story of Moses climbing Mount Sinai to receive the tablets of the Ten Commandments, we learn that the Israelites ran out of patience waiting for Moses to return and built for themselves a golden calf to worship as a god. When God saw what they had done, God wanted to destroy the people and save only Moses. Moses then pleaded that God show mercy and spare their lives. God listened, "and God changed God's mind about the disaster that God planned to bring on God's people" (Exod. 32:14).

Our questions can be a potent source of reflection and prayer. We may enter into Christian service even while we have second thoughts. I have always appreciated the ambiguity of John Shea's wry poem "A Prayer of Wholehearted Commitment." In fact, I included it in my ordination ceremony as a sign that I hadn't always been certain that ministry was the route for me:

Lord,
You have the biblical reputation
of taking people places
they never wanted to go.
Witness Jonah
delivered by whale to Nineveh
and Habakkuk
flown by angel to Babylon.
Also I have heard
You do not consult.
Abraham is suddenly ordered from Haran
and Moses called out of retirement
for the Egypt assignment.
Furthermore
Paul says
You take a chiropodist's delight
in Achilles heels,
spurn eloquence for the stutter,
and reveal yourself
in the thorns of the flesh.

And what was this unpleasantness
with your Son shortly before
his appointment at the Right Hand?
So it is that to You
my most resounding "yes"
is a "maybe"
and it is with one eye on the door
that I say
"Behold, Lord, your servant waiteth."[9]

We may enter into a form of servanthood with certain doubts only to find those questions resolved and others arriving to take their place! Sometimes this is related to our age and maturity, both chronological and spiritual. There is a clear trend in U.S. society for persons to enter ministry at midlife or later, in contrast to the former tradition of starting seminary studies right after completing college. I have heard many of these "second career" people say that they weren't ready for ministry in their twenties or that they heard the call even then but didn't pay attention. Ron Cole-Turner describes calling as a process that changes with each stage of our lives:

> With our basic call in mind, we develop over our whole lifetime a sense of our own special calling. Called first to be Christians, we ask ourselves over and over, from childhood to old age, what specific place we have in the community of Christ and in the mission of the Spirit. As we live, we get an increasingly clearer sense of what our special calling is for each stage of our life.[10]

No matter how life-changing, dramatic, or earth-shaking your sense of calling happened to be, or whether it was a still, small voice or no voice at all that brought you to this work—a motive from the past is not sufficient to carry anyone through the present and future. Your motivation must be a living reality, one that transcends the small defeats of each day, one that enlivens daily life with sacred presence, that helps you to fulfill your transcendent purpose.

≋ Ways to Reassess

There are three criteria, Cole-Turner suggests, that should help us refocus on the purpose of our work. First, we must ask, Is it a mission of the Spirit? Second, does the work match our skills? Do we have the necessary gifts and abilities to fulfill this purpose? Third, is it something that gives us joy? Does it excite the mind, satisfy the spirit, give us moments of timelessness? These questions must be posed not only in moments of private prayer and reflection, but also in a community of the faithful. Discerning whether God is affirming our call or leading us toward a new vocation is better accomplished with the guidance of others who know us and love us.

Renewing our purpose as Christian servants also means looking back and looking forward. In the book *Recalling Our Own Stories: Spiritual Renewal for Religious Caregivers,* Edward Wimberly describes the importance of rehearsing one's call on a regular basis.[11] This allows us to revisit our original sense of purpose and see how far (or not so far) we have come since then. It also allows us to push our vision into the future, when we can more effectively track the trajectory of our faith journey.

The first act in my calling to ministry took place one hot summer night as I walked alone in a small woods. It was late, but I couldn't sleep because my mind was churning. I would soon complete college and was uncertain about my future. I had been working very hard in my courses and had moved around the country several times for internships, so I felt tired and lonely. It seemed something was missing in my life, but I couldn't figure out what it was.

Suddenly, I realized I could do no more on my own. All of my striving and planning had been carried out, and yet I was profoundly unhappy. In that moment, I gave up. It was time for me to recognize my limits and ask for help. And at that moment I knew what I was missing. I fell to my knees in the darkness and, with sand and pine needles as my prayer rug, began to cry. All I could think to ask God was, "Help me, guide me, lead me. I know I have gotten in your way. I have tried to live my life without you. Tonight I know how much I need your presence. Be with me and help me."

I revisit that memory frequently, at times alone and at times in community. There are days when I am back in the same spiritual condition—trying to do it all without God's help or direction. And there are other days when I am able to look back and see how much I have changed since that night of self-surrender. At that time, I had never before actually gotten down on my knees in prayer; I had never revealed my desperation and vulnerability in prayer; I had never even talked aloud to God. That experience was the beginning of a much more personal, dependent, self-revealing relationship with God for me. I recall that night when I counsel someone who is very fragile. I recall it when I am conducting worship and I am deeply touched by God's Spirit and my voice shakes during a prayer. I recall it when I am able to cry openly at weddings and baptisms and funerals. I recall it when I am able to laugh at my own intensity and self-absorption. I recall it when my life seems almost too full of spiritual purpose and meaning, in glaring contrast to those transitional years of my young adulthood. In those moments I know God still waits for me, and God will be patient until I am ready. I know my work today is possible, in part, because of my openness to that time of reckoning with God.

Spiritual conversion is never a purely intellectual proposition. We may make a mental choice at a discrete moment in time, but the choice then must be lived out in the practical details of daily life. We must have an attitude of spiritual openness, which is captured in four lines from another poem by Rainer Maria Rilke, *"Du wirst nur mit der Tat erfasst,"* from a collection of his love poems to God:

> Only in our doing can we grasp you,
> Only with our hands can we illumine you. . . .
> When I go toward you
> it is with my whole life.[12]

≋ Ultimate Purpose

Once we have risen to accept the task of servanthood, how do we then stand? What is our task about? What is our purpose, our mission, our goal?

It is in vogue these days for organizations, committees, and even individuals to write and proclaim their mission statements. This is what we are about; this shows we care; it puts a human face on a large corporation or institution. But more than that, the concept of pursuing a mission is spiritually compelling for people. We want to believe our lives have a plot that is developing in a meaningful way. Human beings are intrinsically fascinated by the details of a personal narrative. Cultures and religious traditions are defined and shaped by their particular stories, fables, or folk tales. One pastoral care writer, Charles Gerkin, has written *The Living Human Document,* which suggests each one of us can be comprehended by his or her "story." A person becomes known by the way she tells her life story and how she derives meaning from it.

Part of the spirituality of servanthood is identifying the ultimate purpose of your story. Articulating your purpose, your vision for the future, is helpful in several ways:

1. It narrows and defines your focus, so you do not waste your energies on marginal tasks.
2. It provides a goal that challenges you to learn more, to open your vision, and to stand in new places.
3. It reassures the people you serve. When you have a clearly articulated purpose, you become a known quantity, someone who can be trusted. You provide a secure foundation as a spiritual companion to others.
4. It offers a reason to persevere when your current situation is less than rewarding.

Defining our purpose in a life of servanthood is both simple and complex. It is simple in that spirituality and spiritual formation are gifts from God the Holy Spirit. All we need to do is to be open to receive the guidance, which will inevitably come through many different streams to form the river that carries us into discipleship. We need not supply this sense of purpose; we are its recipients. The issue is also complex in that we *want* to have a plan, sometimes a detailed one, but living into God's purposes must be an open-ended process. The important thing is that whatever work we choose, it must reflect thankfulness, compassion, love, and service.

Cynthia Robinson described her epiphany as a new mother in an article written for the newsletter of the United Church of Christ Spiritual Development Network:

> At first, I thought that when I began working as a pastor, I would always work as a pastor in a church. And I did, for five years. Now I am a mother and a "pastor" of one: I am helping God to raise a soul. In the process I shall find my own salvation, of that I am sure. When I became pregnant, I said to myself that being a mother would make me a better pastor. Now I am beginning to realize that being a mother is a holy calling in and of itself, and that is enough for today. My path has not changed, only my awareness of it.[13]

≋ The Big Picture

When we combine faith and our life's work, we bring together spirituality and servanthood. At Lifelink, we have a quarterly magazine, and in each issue we profile one staff member and talk about why that person does what he or she does. Some are housing administrators, some are foster care workers, and others are nurses' aides or social workers. I have been impressed by their individual statements of purpose, which are powerful.

"If it wasn't for God in my life, I wouldn't be able to do what I do," said Rosie Johnson, a certified nurse's aide in one of our nursing homes. "This is a ministry to me. It's not just a job. It may be stressful at times, but I believe that I may be doing some good." She has provided hands-on care for many years to persons who can no longer speak or stand. "I like caring for my residents. I like showing them love. They reach out to me and show me love."[14]

Another staff member, Laura Gron, is a Head Start home visitor. She believes that God has sent her the families in her caseload, and she enjoys providing individualized attention to the preschool children and their parents. "There are times when it's hard to see the difference you're making," she admitted. "Sometimes we want things for the parents more than they want it for themselves. But the reward comes in seeing changes happen over two or three years, watching parents become more independent and work toward some goals. I really feel I see my families through Christ's eyes. I hope they feel His love, mercy and compassion through me."[15]

Amos Bradford, the administrator of a Chicago housing residence for physically disabled adults and senior citizens, described his goal as helping those in his care "to strive to attain higher heights. We invite God into our work here. We serve Him as we serve others." His religious calling allows him to keep reaching out to his physically challenged residents, who are victims of gunshot wounds and accidents or have genetic diseases, and to older adults with limited resources.[16]

One of Lifelink's foster care staff was brought into this challenging field as a direct result of prayer. Having completed a law degree, Sanford Jaffe asked God what he should do with his education. God then led him to Chicago and a job as a licensing representative. "I'm here for a specific purpose and I have a vision for this job," said Jaffe, who fervently described his commitment to seeing that children have a good home and God's trustworthiness. "Without religious faith and a sense of God's direction, I would have burned out a long time ago."[17]

I am reminded of the words of a Hebrew prophet, which many Christians have adopted as their statement of purpose:

> What does God require of you,
> but to do justice, and to love kindness,
> and to walk humbly with your God? (Mic. 6:8)

Finally, examining our purpose must make sense in the broader scheme of life. How is our individual purpose serving God's broader purpose? How does our work glorify God? How does it bring God's dominion to earth? How does it connect with the liturgical story? What does it do to heal our alienation, the breach between God and humankind? Does your faith allow you to act on Monday in a way that reflects what happened in church on Sunday? It should, and if it does not, one or the other needs to change. In one church, the congregation faces the door at the close of worship, and the pastor offers this benediction: "Our service is over, but the work of God is just beginning."

Why we do what we do is important on several levels: it is crucial for the people we serve; it is important to our sense of vocation; and it is an essential element of bringing mercy and justice to the wider society. In a lecture given at Lifelink, Dr. Michael Welker of Heidelberg University in Germany underscored the biblical mandate given to institutions of diakonal ministry:

> The Old Testament law traditions see very clearly that the inclinations and actions which they call "mercy" are not only important to the recipients, but are also of benefit to the whole society. "Mercy" is the devotion to the weak, to the strangers, the widows, the orphans, the persecuted, and to those who are in the minority. Without continuous mercy, that is, the institutionalized readiness to help the weak and the frail, a society degenerates and the social system becomes more and more brutalized and defensive.[18]

Jesus asks that we carry out our purpose *wherever we are,* not flailing away in all directions, not looking to the past or the future constantly and missing the opportunities in this present hour. I have reflected often on Jesus' words in Luke 9:62: "No one who puts a hand to the plow and looks back is fit for the kingdom of God." Our vocation and purpose have no meaning unless they become real right here and right now. This is truly what it means to practice the resurrection: to know that God is with us in this moment of time; that the Spirit fills us in this very room; that wherever two or three are gathered, Christ is there in the midst of them. Thanks be to God.

≈ **4**

Personal Discipline as a
Fearsome Prospect

O'erthrow me.
　　　—*John Donne*

≈ Make Connections

How then is this done, the life of spirituality in diakonal ministry?
What do we do to sustain our spirits? Is it something we can talk
about? I would venture a guess that most of us are not skilled in the
inner life, that most of our lives are lived on the rational, intellectual level, that we are threatened by the mysterious and paradoxical terrain of the heart and soul. Yet if one of our goals as
Christians is to achieve wholeness, we must be able to integrate our
inner and outer worlds. There must be a way for the private and
public realms of our lives to intersect and cohere. This spiritual
exploration allows us to tap into God-given resources of hope and
healing, and it enables us to feel connections with others who are
on the same journey.

Perhaps we are afraid of this prospect, for many of us avoid deep
engagement in spirituality as we carry out our ministry of Christian
service. We quite conventionally divide ourselves into Marys and
Marthas, believing that we must live either as a sheltered contem-
plative like Mary or as a busy doer of good works like Martha
(Luke 10:38–42). If we kneel at Jesus' feet to listen as Mary did, we
will not have time to put on the apron of hospitality. If we are
caught up in stocking the pantry for the soup kitchen like Martha,

we will begin to feel that this work in itself is prayer and we need not wait for mystical visions. For centuries, Christians have taken sides as to which kind of life is morally superior or have at least concluded that Mary and Martha each chose a useful path. Yet each woman needed the challenge posed by the other. Why should either of the sisters have been content in a one-sided role? Both spirituality and service, contemplation and action, are needed for our souls and for the work of God's dominion.

In my religious life, I was raised in the "Mary" mode. The preaching and teaching in the church of my youth were theologically sound but mostly inwardly directed, with a focus on God's acceptance of each person as an individual and an understanding of personal psychological strengths and weaknesses in light of Christian faith. As I grew older, I could tell that my pastor was preaching to himself in many ways (now I realize we all do!). It seemed he had grown up with a lot of shame, not feeling he was good enough, and he found the ability to love himself only through God's grace. Certainly, that was an authentic message from the gospel, and I was able to integrate it into my struggles with identity and belief. But as a young person also vitally interested in politics and social justice, I never would have entered a religious vocation had it not been for a university chaplain who showed me that Christians also can be at the forefront of change in society. Since I had been raised with a very individualistic faith, a revelation for me was to learn that the church actually had a meaningful role in the broader culture and that Christian organizations were taking prophetic stands on controversial social issues. It finally made sense to me that I could integrate my personal beliefs and my public actions.

The lure of the "Martha" mode of service is knowing that you are accomplishing something worthwhile. Martha knew the food had to get on the table and somebody needed to make sure it got there. People could sit and talk to Jesus all day, but eventually, they would get hungry; the body cannot be sustained by spiritual food alone. Furthermore, hospitality is a significant form of Christian ministry. Extending welcome, caring, and love through food and shelter is an expression of the good news. Martha also embodies the protester or activist; she did not hesitate to confront Jesus about her anger and sense of injustice. But Martha's complaint about Mary also points out the danger of a life primarily focused on doing rather than being. Even righteous action can tire us out over time, and if we do not stop periodically to reflect on our greater purpose, we may become resentful and lose any connection to the spiritual meaning of our work.

Donne's poetic plea is that God use force to break through to him, to open the storehouse and bring new wisdom. Like Donne, we need God to initiate the challenge, for our resistance is strong. Most of us prefer comfort if we can find it, and we build spiritual and psychological defenses to shore up our sense of security. We choose the path of Mary or Martha. Often unexpected events outside our control force us to change. These disruptive experiences in many cases may be God's way of moving us from our cherished complacency to growth in grace. I can envision a later installment in the story of Mary and Martha, in which Martha is taking a three-day retreat in the desert to pray and Mary is organizing a clothing drive in Bethany. This turn of events would lead both of them to more fulfillment as whole persons created in God's image.

The poet David Whyte addresses our fear of examining the inner life in his books, including *The Heart Aroused: Poetry and the Preservation of the Soul in Corporate America.*[1] He uses poetry as a means of breaking open the spiritual truth contained within our souls. Whyte believes that most of us have learned to hide the soul's depths from others, creating "a kind of inner Stealth technology so you don't appear on life's radar screen" and thus cannot be hurt. "But there's a tremendous cost to that. One of the costs is that not only are other people unable to recognize you, but you get to the place where you cannot recognize yourself."[2]

Whyte suggests that poetry allows us to open up the soul's voice, to examine the shadows that we fear as well as our sense of belonging. This spiritual awareness is basically developed through paying attention to what is living around us and inside us. To come to know what is happening in our souls, we must unburden ourselves, surrender our control, and explore what is deep, textured, mysterious, and what makes sense to us in a celebratory way. Whyte advises that we will become better acquainted with our spirits in the places where we have a sense of belonging. If we are fortunate to feel we "belong" to a worshiping community, a workplace, a neighborhood, a family, or a group of other souls, we will find our true passions and our true gifts. This search becomes a spiritual discipline in itself as each of us looks for a voice, a story, and develops the courage to speak.

≋ Begin Where You Are

Many of us understand the prospect of spiritual discipline as something we must escape from ordinary life to find. Yet few of us have this choice to make, and there is no need for us to escape to a desert island or some higher spiritual plane.

> Human beings don't get to choose between making a living—making the car payments and mortgage payments and college fees—and living out their destiny. . . . I don't think God is impressed with our arguments that we can refuse to live out our destiny because we happen to be earning a living at the time.[3]

We need not hide the soul while we get through the "dailyness" of life. This is exactly where we need to bring it out, examining our successes and our failures, living with our whole hearts. Some of us may hide the soul's truth because we are afraid, but others can immobilize the soul through busyness, a way of hiding from others and hiding from oneself that produces exhaustion. Oh, for the gift to see ourselves as others see us!

Whyte shares a story of a time when he was caught up in a whirl-wind of activity and approached a good friend, Brother David

Steindl-Rast, asking for advice about his tiredness: "The antidote to exhaustion is not necessarily rest. It's wholeheartedness. Your discipline now is to move toward things you can do wholeheartedly."[4] When we are not sure about taking on a new commitment, perhaps we need to ask, Is this task obligation or inspiration? Stopping to answer a basic question like this one is a way of practicing spiritual discipline in and through the choices we constantly face.

Spirituality moves us in the direction of pursuits that are most life-giving to us, but as human beings we may approach this path with fear and trembling. At this point I should offer a definition of spirituality, particularly as it pertains to a life of service. Christian spirituality is a gift from God. It is the way that God works in our lives to enable us to be conscious of spiritual realities and to establish deeper relationships with God and other people. We cannot buy it in a pill or a package. We cannot earn it by good works or analyze it with technology. We can learn more about spirituality by developing our awareness through a variety of means, many of which are described in chapter 7.

Spirituality gives us an identity that is transcendent and eternal. It is the living sense that we are, through faith, the people of God, disciples of Jesus Christ, and instruments of the Holy Spirit. The power of spirituality teaches us that we are part of something larger than ourselves. It calls us into gathered communities for worship, into private experiences of wonder and awe, and into service on behalf of our brothers and sisters. We acknowledge our deep humility and utter dependence upon God as spiritual persons and are given at the same time tremendous power and the willingness to be interdependent with our brothers and sisters in faith.

Spirituality is not something we create by doing "spiritual" things. *It is the work of God*, and as human beings we all have a human spirit. Spirituality is learning to receive God's Spirit, to experience and know God in many life experiences. It is available to all people, from birth to death. The spiritual wonder and openness many children display cause them to be spiritual teachers for adults. Spirituality is accessible to all people, regardless of physical or mental capabilities. Persons who may be paralyzed or cannot hear or see often have a very keen spiritual awareness and insight.

In recent years there has been a fast-growing interest in spirituality. Some of it has developed within the church, but many spiritual books today have little or no connection with the institutional church. This is possible because spirituality and religion are not the same, although clearly they are interconnected. Spirituality is a way of being, a form of awareness, an experience of religious power, as I have described it here. Religion, in contrast, is a set of beliefs and principles that emerge from a faith story. Religion is defined by historical events, theology, confessions, creeds, and statements of faith, and it is generally vested in an institution of some kind. Religion gives rise to traditions, rituals, practices, and testaments that describe the truth about life, death, and transcendent meaning. Religion also gives birth to various kinds of spiritual traditions: Catholic spirituality has given us icons, images, grottoes, and shrines; Protestant spirituality is typically more focused on words and music than on religious symbols. Depending upon your point of view, spirituality can be seen as only one form of religious expression or as a reality that completely encompasses and even goes beyond the world of religion.

In the past, religion was a more central and normative part of daily life and culture. Spiritual values were naturally woven into community traditions, such as serving fish on Friday in public schools (honoring a form of fasting) or closing stores on Sunday (honoring the need for Sabbath rest). Today, many of our communities are more religiously diverse, and religious values have been separated from mainstream culture. Nonetheless, the human soul demands nurture, and so now people turn to the popular media for spiritual resources—sometimes overlooking what is available to them through the institutional church. Many are seeking a spirituality that is compatible with today's fast-paced, stressful lifestyle, which unfortunately minimizes the true value of Christian spiritual life. John Shea talked about this in the lecture "Spirituality Outside the Churches." He says people want spirituality to be a means of increasing their productivity, managing more information, and maintaining the ability to move quickly and be excellent. But they want all this without paying the price, without slowing down, without making a covenantal commitment to be a faithful member of a Christian community. He questions whether it is possible to achieve a meaningful spirituality without taking time to go deep, to rest for a moment, before again taking up the struggle.[5]

One of my concerns is that for many well-intentioned persons the spiritual quest is being tarnished by our society's prevalent consumer mentality. We rob spirituality of its life's blood when we divorce it from a religious tradition. Spiritual resources may be found in the psychology or self-help sections of bookstores. Sometimes people "shop around" for a church or a spiritual discipline that "meets my needs" rather than see that we are called to *conform ourselves* to spiritual life. It is also dangerous to assume that certain elements of a religious tradition could be disposable—another common attitude in our convenience-oriented society. We take what we like and ignore the things that don't fit our lifestyle, creating a do-it-yourself spirituality.

Spiritual life is a natural outgrowth or expression of religious belief and practice. It must be founded upon religious teachings so that believers have a resource for both comfort and correction when the spiritual pilgrimage becomes hard to navigate. People who are spiritual without being religious will at some point sail alone through frightening waters, with no safe shelter. People who are religious without being spiritual will dwell on the intellectual, rule-based content of faith and miss the *lived experience* of being in relationship with God.

≋ Take the Time

Beginning to practice a spiritual discipline requires the one thing we believe is most valuable to us: time. Many of us have learned through experience that the best way to feed the inner life is to take time for it. Actually, a better description would be that we need to give God the time to feed our souls. Listening for God, giving God the opportunity to overthrow our worldly habits and ideas, requires commitment. However, time is a precious commodity, and we may confuse *serving* God and *being with* God. They are not always one and the same.

I know Christian servants who feel the best response to their call is to work hard. "If I am not working or being productive, I have no value," the inner voice maintains. The measure of your worth and effectiveness is how busy you are, how overextended you have become. In fact, this is not a religious way to measure human worth. It has no relationship to listening for God. Christian service is not about productivity, busyness, or even goodness as a person. Edward Wimberly addresses this concern:

> Something keeps us walking wounded from working on our own needs. Sometimes it is related to images of perfection. At other times, we lack recognition of our own need for care and nurture. We don't feel we have permission to take time to care for our own needs. So we never learn to transform our own woundedness into a resource to be used in caring. As walking wounded and wounded healers, we need times of retreat and care to tend to our own needs so that we can return to the caring task of providing good enough empathy.[6]

At the heart of our work is the worship of God, not moralistic perfection to "be the best." It is okay to enjoy our work! Servanthood should not make us feel like slaves. Don't we sometimes feel that if our work is awful and involves tremendous self-sacrifice, then it must be God's will? In fact, if we are unhappy in one form of service, it may be a sign that God is calling us to something else. Servant ministry comes from God, not the servant. This also helps us in moments when we wonder whether the people we are serving actually merit our love. The basic question of *diakonia* is not whether the neighbor needs our love, but whether we are capable of sharing God's love. If we are miserable, we are probably not sharing anybody's love.

An alternative view of servanthood is to see that the work of spiritual life is just as important as the work we do "at work." I am reminded of the title of a recent book on Buddhist meditation: *Don't Just Do Something, Sit There.* If we fail to devote time to spiritual self-nurture and critical reflection, our work will eventually be emptied of its spiritual power. Too many of us work hard, then drop. We need to give the body, mind, and spirit time to lie fallow before plowing the earth and seeding a new crop. Richard Baxter described in the 1655 book *The Reformed Pastor* the perils of trying to lead people when we have run out of inspiration. His message remains contemporary for clergy or laity:

> When I let my heart grow cold, my preaching is cold; and when it is confused, my preaching will be so; and so I can observe too oft in the best of my hearers, that when I have a while grown cold in preaching, they have cooled accordingly, and the next prayers which I have heard from them have been too like my preaching. We are the nurses of Christ's little ones. . . . If we let our love go down we are not likely to raise up theirs.[7]

Baxter's recommendation is that a pastor be rekindled in soul through private prayer and meditation, time spent with God, and reading books that inspire. Baxter was a spiritual person who first of all paid attention to his life before God and then looked at the conditions of his parishioners' souls. The word "discipline" unfortunately carries many negative connotations today. We feel a vague fear and hesitancy about spiritual discipline, associating it with monks and nuns in a cloister. The word "discipline" itself reminds us of deprivation rather than self-nurture. It is also a word we use synonymously with "punishment," as when a parent threatens a disobedient child with the prospect of "discipline." For most of us mainstream Protestants, spiritual discipline seems to have little or no connection to the reality in which we live.

In today's world, the tracks of workaholism are more familiar—albeit self-destructive—paths to follow. Persons who are geared toward organization and accomplishment find spiritual pursuits frustrating, and feel that disciplines such as meditation and retreats are wastes of time because nothing outwardly gets done.

But one pastor I know discovered that staying busy with meetings, visits, and administrative work left him with a feeling that something vital was missing. And he knew the answer was not a new seminar or pastoral technique. He realized his spirit was restless, and he made a deliberate decision to invest time in spiritual reading, a soul friend, and a journal. As he began this new regimen, the minister found himself having to reschedule certain meetings and appointments around the time he set aside for his soul work. Because the pastor now feels this time is essential to his vocation, he puts it in his weekly schedule alongside other responsibilities. It has given him the feeling, he says, that he has taken control—or allowed Another to take control—of his life and ministry.

≈≈ Rekindle the Soul

We need mentors and spiritual friends to teach us the value of reading poetry, praying with our coworkers, sharing devotional times in the family, or participating in Bible study. Finding spiritual companions for these pursuits also takes time and energy. The pastor I just described looked long and hard for a soul friend before finding that person through a monthly support group. The two then met weekly to talk and pray, and they held each other accountable to finish the books they wanted to read or to make the time to journal. (See chapter 6 for other ways to create spiritual community.)

Doing these things in a consistent way can reveal to us the implicit spiritual challenges and gifts in our work of service. I appreciate many of the questions Matthew Fox included in a "Spirituality of Work" survey in his book *The Re-invention of Work*. They call us to measure the spiritual value and content of our efforts, to consider how our service affects both inward and outward life. Fox asks us to ask ourselves:

Do I experience joy in my work?

Do others experience joy as a result of my work?

Is my work actively creating good work for others?

When did I first feel drawn to the kind of work I am doing?

How is my work a blessing to generations to come?

How am I emptied at work?

What inner work have I been involved in over the last five years?

How does my work affect the environment?

Are awe and wonder experienced in my work?

Am I growing younger every day?

What is the funniest thing about my work?

What is sacred about the work I do?[8]

As intentional Christian servants, we actually need more than the minimum requirement of one hour of worship each week. Because our souls are shaped by our experiences of servanthood, going to church is certainly not the only (or even the best) spiritually nourishing activity for us. A support group, prayer group, recovery group, spiritual direction group, healing service, house church, or peer group may become more meaningful to us than traditional congregational worship. In addition, many clergy have little opportunity to be worshipers since they are usually the worship leaders. Our spiritual needs cannot be set aside until we get to that one conference or vacation per year. Attending to the inner life should be as typical a daily activity as eating, sleeping, or working.

Again, we must be wary of temptation. We cannot make ourselves more spiritual purely by dint of our efforts. Spiritual growth cannot be forced. Disciplines of faith are a way we can respond to God's work with gratitude; they are not another shallow self-improvement project or form of self-pampering. Even spirituality has been co-opted by secular culture, and I have seen several articles that describe prayer and meditation merely as ways to cope with stress (when they are much more than this) and equate disciplines of faith with yoga or massage as a means to relaxation. A paper on spirituality written by the faculty of United Church of Christ–related Eden Theological Seminary notes this concern, pointing out that in contemporary American culture fasting as a spiritual discipline is dangerous since it could turn into another form of dieting for many Christians.[9] Spending time on spiritual disciplines will not always make us feel nurtured or relaxed. It will not always feel like an escape because often we examine something in daily life more deeply or carefully after prayer or spiritual direction. The goal of the spiritual quest is not instant happiness but mature wisdom.

≈ Gain New Perspective

How can the power of spirituality transform our culturally dominated ways of thinking? John Shea offers four insightful observations.[10] First, spirituality reminds us that the Spirit is always present, but we are the ones who are absent. We don't have to go out and get it. Spirituality is always within us, and all we need to do is wake up to its presence. For some people, this happens overnight. Bob, who had faithfully attended church all of his life, finally discovered that Christianity actually had an effect on his life when he wound up in the hospital after having a heart attack at age forty-five. Suddenly, prayers and Scripture had a new reality for him, and Bob became personally involved in spirituality rather than hearing about it from a pew.

Denise Levertov, in the eloquent poem "Flickering Mind," describes our feeble attempts to remain present and aware of God:

> Lord, not you,
> it is I who am absent.
> At first
> belief was a joy I kept in secret,
> stealing alone

into sacred places:
a quick glance, and away—and back,
circling.
I have long since uttered your name
but now
I elude your presence.
I stop
to think about you, and my mind
at once
like a minnow darts away,
darts
into the shadows, into gleams that fret
unceasing over
the river's purling and passing.
Not for one second
will my self hold still, but wanders
anywhere,
everywhere it can turn. Not you,
it is I am absent.
You are the stream, the fish, the light,
the pulsing shadow,
you the unchanging presence, in whom all
moves and changes.
How can I focus my flickering, perceive
at the fountain's heart
the sapphire I know is there?[11]

Spiritual meaning is not far away. We need not climb mountains or search for it to the ends of the earth. We are surrounded by God; but it does take some effort for our eyes to be opened.

Second, spirituality teaches us that everything is grist for the mill. Successes and failures are both essential to human living. Above and below all that we do in life is the goal of becoming more spiritually developed, and this happens through the good and the bad. Experiences of suffering may not be reflections of God's punishment, but they may hold within them a call to repentance and new life. I find many Christians continue to hold the belief that having a bad experience is God's way of taking revenge for something they did wrong in the past.

Jesus addressed this concern as he talked with his disciples after meeting a man who was blind from birth (John 9:1–12). The disciples asked Jesus whether the man had been born blind because of his own sin or his parents' sin. Jesus strongly disagreed that the man's blindness was a result of sin. Instead, Jesus said his condition was an opportunity for God's works to be revealed. Jesus then spat on the ground, mixing his saliva with dust, spread the mud on the blind man's eyes, and asked him to go wash in the pool of Siloam. The man did so and received his sight. Our attention is shifted from the *cause* of the disability to its *spiritual purpose*. The experience of suffering in human life is an opportunity for God to act.

David Whyte believes successes and failures in our lives are like the waxing and waning of the moon, simply cycles of change: "The very beauty of the moon is its coming and going. Yet we have no patience for our own coming and going."[12] Life transitions can be confusing until we discover that the changes can bring new meaning. Everything, including experiences of the absence of God, can have spiritual purpose.

Third, spirituality insists on our need for reflection and contemplation. Most of us live in a world that requires our attention and awareness to be focused outside ourselves every hour of the day except when we are sleeping. We tire easily when our consciousness is always outwardly directed; meditation pulls our attention back inside the soul, where we can feel the energy of life renew us. Meditation does not necessarily mean we need to sit on a floor pillow with our legs crossed and eyes closed. Some people meditate by journaling, doing physical work, or taking a bubble bath. The outward form may be different for each of us, but the inner work is the same.

Occasionally, I will stay for one night at a retreat center near my home. I go alone, with no agenda except sleeping, reading, and writing. There is no telephone in the room, no TV or radio, no food or alcohol or any of the usual forms of distraction we usually count on to induce relaxation. There is sheer silence, pure quiet. Accustomed as I am to using music or entertainment to relax, I am always amazed that I am still capable of sitting in silence and allowing my body and soul to find peace and quiet without any external aids. During these solitary retreats, usually less than twenty-four hours long, I repeatedly experience the temptation to resort to food or drink or some busy occupation as a quick route to relaxation. For me, this spiritual retreat time is not just a coping mechanism, but a way of finding my true self again, recovering who I am as God's beloved without all the accoutrements of modern life. I can return to my magazines and videos with the reassurance that I do enjoy them but that I could also live without them.

Fourth, Shea says, God's Spirit is immanent, and prayer, liturgy, and ritual help us to go within ourselves to find God. Even so, the Spirit is not easily domesticated. Shea takes issue with the New Age form of syncretistic spiritualities that would treat spiritual life as a household god you keep around and use when you like it. "People don't harness Spirit, as if we were equals. It's not so docile, you can't put it on a leash. You can't put it to work for you. You work for it."[13] He also reiterates the need for community discernment and discipline for anyone who is seriously following a spiritual path. Both are needed to correct the temptation toward individualism, and the danger that the greedy ego will prevail. Susan Howatch has written a series of popular novels on the theme of pastors with strong spiritual gifts and insights who nevertheless often used their abilities in ways that harmed themselves and others. These books, including *Absolute Powers* and *Glittering Images,* trace the lives of clergy from the Anglican Church who rely upon spiritual directors and companions to ensure that they will use their God-given abilities for God's purposes and not their own.

When we are truly connected to the Spirit within, we have the ability to act more freely. We are not simply reacting to what is going on outside us. We are proactive, guided by the light within that emerges naturally from the true self.

≈ Go on a Pilgrimage

Discipline creates a habit, a way of being. Though we may have to intentionally commit ourselves to engage in spiritual discipline if it is not part of our custom or tradition, it should not long remain something we have to force ourselves to do in an unpleasant way. Engaging in spiritual discipline should not be like going on a diet: we know it's good for us, but it involves a lot of deprivation. Eventually, the practice should become a natural part of who we are and the way we live.

In the United Church of Christ, we have an inspiring tradition of spiritual discipline that can be uncovered in the history of Puritan piety. Reading through some of the early spiritual journals of our mothers and fathers in faith, I was struck by the fact that the church completely shaped the life of each believer. Worship was not something to be squeezed in for an hour on Sunday. Instead, life itself was a form of worship, and all other work and activities of life fit into this spiritual framework.

Many Puritans engaged in numerous forms of spiritual discipline: godly conversation with other persons of faith; Sabbath rest; fasting; thanksgiving; religious lectures; group worship that occupied most of each Sunday; morning and evening devotions with the family; talks and thoughts upon spiritual matters; acts of charity; and "many scores of ejaculations each day in whatever place we come into."[14] Let me hasten to clarify that these ejaculations were spiritual outcries of joy and praise, some spoken aloud and others uttered silently.

Recovering in the contemporary world this complete devotion to godly things is nearly impossible for us, and it would not necessarily be desirable anyway. Preparation for death and eternity was perhaps an overly prominent theme in the Puritans' daily life. Religious anxiety was a prevalent motivating force, to what we would now see as an unhealthy degree. But many of these spiritual practices and understandings are easily transferable to the life of a modern-day Christian servant. Certainly, we have retained the idea that life is a pilgrimage through this world, a journey of the soul to be joined in complete union with God. We still observe the belief that God does not come *because* we engage in a certain religious exercise, but that if God is going to come into our awareness, God will do so through the means of that exercise.

The United Church of Christ in 1995 published the booklet *Friends of God and Prophets,* which offers several practical spiritual exercises for persons who are working for compassion and justice in the world. The suggested practices, such as focusing on breathing, being attentive, journaling, doing spiritual reading, and meditating, are all habits of the early Congregationalists.[15] I commend the book to anyone engaged in a life of service. Each generation and each individual must relearn and retranslate these practices, to discover new ways of covenanting with God.

≋ Heed a Warning

Immersion in disciplines of faith is not just a wholesome habit. Someone who is seriously engaged in Christian service will find that life becomes a daily battle against the forces of evil, within and without. Strengthening your soul is a necessary precaution against these threatening forces, which can harm you in body and spirit. You may be confronting a corrupt system, a pattern of pervasive evil, threats of brutality or even death. That you are facing this trial may not mean your spiritual work has gone astray; instead, it may indicate that you have delved to the heart of a crucial problem. That you live always in a sinful world should not defeat your purposes, but inform them. As William Stringfellow describes it: "Biblical spirituality concerns living in the midst of the era of the Fall, wherein all relationships whatsoever have been lost or damaged or diminished or twisted or broken, in a way which is open to the transcendence of the fallenness of each and every relationship and in which these very relationships are recovered or rendered new."[16]

Stringfellow also warns Christians against following any spirituality that promotes nonbiblical values, such as the pursuit of success or celebrity, the worship of nothing, immediate gratification replacing hope, or self-denial that becomes self-gratification. Many old and new forms of worship and spirituality tempt us to depart from true faith by pursuing these seductive, but false, ideals.

≋ Keep Hope Alive

Acknowledging the power of evil in our world liberates us to face life with resilient, unflinching realism. To expect opposition and barriers to God's work is to be appropriately prepared for what will come, so our minds are not clouded by sentimental illusions. Such an outlook paradoxically protects us from utter disillusionment. When we understand sinfulness to be part of the human condition, our philosophy cannot be demolished by "the disappointing facts of human history," in the words of Reinhold Niebuhr:

> It is tremendously difficult, without the paradoxes of religion, to escape estimates of human nature which betray into absurdity by their consistency. . . . In the insights of the Christian religion and the poetic symbolism of all true religion, man is first driven to despair by the knowledge of his sins and then encouraged by the hope that redemption is possible for him. He finds life tragic but also worth living, because he beholds the beauty in the tragedy.[17]

Only through the practice of rigorous disciplines can we escape cynicism and sentimentalism and remain spiritually alive to continue serving.

At the same time, it is not our calling to accept evil, for such acceptance tends to deaden our moral sensitivity and create inertia. "It's too big. I can't do anything to change it. I'll just learn to live with it." Even when our voices are in the smallest minority, we must not compromise by remaining silent. Public witness will always be an outgrowth of spiritual discipline. This, too, can be a fearsome prospect for some who would rather sit in the back row and not start an argument. In his book *Engaging the Powers,* Walter Wink advises Christians to combine prayer and action and call evil by its name: "Naming as evil what others regard as custom (wife beating) or natural (homophobia) or even moral (executing political critics or religious heretics)—maintains the moral nerve even in circumstances where change seems impossible."[18]

Nothing else but religious faith can provide us with sufficient strength to maintain "courage in the struggle for justice and peace," to quote the United Church of Christ Statement of Faith.

Who or what is our enemy? What makes our journey as caring people such a struggle? We may identify it as evil people, or a severely flawed system, apathy, inertia, ignorance, or a range of other seemingly intractable problems. But it may also be true that our greatest enemy is a failure to lead and to act with Christian conviction in spite of these obstacles. God knows we often long for the world to be different than it is. We have a long litany of "if only's." If only there were more people of good will to help us. If only we had more money. If only the church could move more quickly. If only the person we're trying to care for would listen to what we're saying. If only our leaders could act with moral integrity. If only these situations would change, then we could truly make a difference. Until then, we continue to focus blame on what is outside ourselves and do not reflect upon the enemy within. The discipline of critical reflection on our own lives must be part of the spirituality of those who seek to serve others, for one of our enemies is the temptation to be self-righteous.

We are called to live with moral courage in a broken world, acknowledging our own limits. How can this bring us hope? Robert K. Greenleaf, a Quaker and leader in the field of business management and ethics, urges those who see themselves as faithful servants to fuse their sense of humility and devotion with the authority of leadership. Concerned about the dissolving credibility of many traditional institutions (such as churches, universities, and corporations), he wrote several books on the theme of "servant leadership." In his view, leaders who serve the needs and gifts of the people within their own organizations—rather than serving their own desires for power, wealth, or ambition—are the only means of saving these havens of hope in an imperfect world. His fear is that people who are natural servants will hesitate to assume positions of authority because they will not want to sully their ideals in the muddy waters of real world decision making. Greenleaf believes that servant leadership will always require personal discipline because it aims toward an ideal community which will never be fully realized, and he acknowledges that sometimes our greatest struggle is simply to persevere.[19]

To summarize: We are afraid of the prospect of spiritual discipline. We are afraid it would claim too much of our lives, we are afraid it would change us, or we are afraid that we will fail. Discipline is in many ways a foreign concept for us in contemporary times, and it flies in the face of a consumerist culture. Nevertheless, we confront enemies within and without that we are powerless to overcome if we do not have a strong spiritual core. If we seek to lead and to serve, we need to put aside our fears (after acknowledging that they are real) and honor the soul's calling. In these times, I reflect on another piece of wisdom from Niebuhr:

> Nothing that is worth doing can be achieved in our lifetime; therefore we must be saved by hope. Nothing which is true or beautiful or good makes complete sense in any immediate context of history; therefore we must be saved by faith. Nothing we do, however virtuous, can be accomplished alone; therefore we must be saved by love. No virtuous act is quite as virtuous from the standpoint of our friend or foe as it is from our standpoint. Therefore we must be saved by the final form of love which is forgiveness.[20]

≋ **5**

Obedience Lessons for Leaders

Bend your force to break, blow, burn.

—John Donne

Leaders in ministry often need obedience lessons as we engage in the work of spiritual life. Learning to submit the will and purpose to God is a paradoxical challenge for us, because though our work is termed "servanthood," our daily responsibilities demand leadership. Following God's leading while investing ourselves in the practicalities of program, budget, staffing, and support is a tough balancing act. The common perception is that an individual is either a leader or a follower, a visionary or a worker (like the Mary/Martha dichotomy discussed earlier).

Yet biblical examples reveal that God discloses a greater, more holistic vision to persons who are engaged in both spirituality and practical service. For instance, Jesus called several fishermen to be his disciples, challenging them to take the skills learned through boats and nets to begin to "fish for people" (Matt. 4:19). Jesus said a shepherd's task, at that time considered a lowly occupation, had parallels to nurturing and feeding a community of people and called himself "the good shepherd" (John 10:14). To the Samaritan woman who drew water from the well to slake Jesus' thirst, he explained that his gift was to provide "living water" (John 4:10).

≋ **Listening**

How then do we infuse our pragmatic responsibilities with a spirit of holy obedience? How will we allow God's force to bend our conventions and traditions in a way that breaks open new meaning and new life?

Let's start with meetings. It seems that little can be accomplished in the world of diakonal ministry without hours and hours spent sitting in meetings. Often I dread them, sometimes I actually gain something from them, but generally I view them as unavoidable necessities of church and work life. The words, "We need to schedule a meeting," cause me to inwardly shudder. Can the world of meetings somehow be infused with soul and transformed into an experience of obedience? How might this happen? Consider one scenario.

A meeting of the All Saints Church board of trustees is called for Thursday night. The first issue on the agenda is deciding how to participate in a community food pantry. St. Pius Church is running out of room to house the pantry, the community center does not want to accept the liability of the program, and no other church in town is willing to take on the responsibility of administration and oversight. One trustee is ready for a fight, in strong opposition to using one of the All Saints' Christian education classrooms for the pantry. Two others are known in advance to be pushing in favor of the program. The source of funds for any needed renovation is unclear. The pastor is out of town and won't be able to attend on Thursday. These are all the practical and political concerns. Here is how a "theology of meetings" might be enacted.

The chairperson, Susan, begins the meeting with a reading of two Scripture passages about feeding the hungry. She then asks for a few minutes of silence, inviting each person to pray or meditate on the biblical words and to listen for God's leading in them. Following the quiet time, Susan asks the members to share whatever thoughts or leadings they have had. Some people are surprised by the moving of the Spirit within them; others choose not to say anything and perhaps felt nothing. Susan urges respect for others' ideas, even if there is disagreement. Then there is a group prayer, asking God to lead the trustees to a faithful decision. The discussion continues, exploring the community's emergency food needs and whether it is All Saints' calling to meet them.

Susan reminds the trustees of the church's mission and vision statement written two years ago, which includes a clear call to local, hands-on service. Members share stories of their experiences with hunger and poverty, as well as Bible verses and prayers that inform their thinking about this situation. One person addresses what educational ministries would be gained and lost if the church had one less classroom available. Another trustee describes the financial requirements of the effort in terms of stewardship needs and opportunities. Before the vote is taken, Susan asks again for a few minutes of silent prayer. The trustees make their final decision by consensus.

A dream meeting? Certainly it is. And I would hope that the trustees did not overlook any pragmatic realities of the proposal because their primary attention was given to the genuine emotions and faith claims that were shared. A meeting like this is within the realm of possibility if we are able to reenvision our service as both obeying God's voice and listening to our own wisdom and experience. In fact, "obedience" means "listening deeply." If we truly examine our typical participation in meetings, we may discover that we are motivated by self-interest, competition, fear of embarrassment, desire for cooperation, need for approval, and many other very human—but not necessarily spiritual—attitudes. What happens when we are able to see the experience of the meeting *itself* as an opportunity for service?

Robert Greenleaf developed the term "servant-leader" for the person who is able to embody both obedience and leadership in using authority. He describes a servant-leader as someone who is a "servant-first" rather than being a "leader-first":

> The difference manifests itself in the care taken by the servant-first to make sure that other people's highest priority needs are being served. The best test, and difficult to administer, is: Do those served grow as persons? Do they, *while being served,*

become healthier, wiser, freer, more autonomous, more likely themselves to become servants? And, what is the effect on the least privileged in society; will they benefit, or, at least, not be further deprived?[1]

Obedience in leadership is practiced not only by listening for God's guidance, but also by listening to those being served, understanding that this is essential to what God wants for us as servant-leaders. It demands awareness, a spiritual quality of consciousness that acknowledges there is more going on in a given situation than is revealed on the surface.

Many times I have been brought up short when I have taken the time to ask the people I serve what *they* want instead of presuming that *I* know best. They do not want me to be serious all the time—they want me to have a sense of humor. They do not want Bible study primarily for spiritual guidance—they want intellectual stimulation and the challenge of learning about historical and literary criticism of the Bible. They do not want me to be the expert on ethics—they want to bring their experiences to the table for discussion. I have also learned that when I am praying with someone, the most important question to ask is, "What do *you* want me to pray for today?" The nature of the prayer requests is often much different from what I would have guessed. A servant always stops to ask for directions.

≋ Living on Two Levels

Discerning the difference between our authority and God's authority is a significant spiritual lesson that we must relearn repeatedly. Is this new project something God would have us do, or just an idea that would give us power and boost the ego? Is it time to quit this job because God has something else in mind for us, or just so we can escape the conflict? Once we have learned to listen for God, once we have given priority to spiritual realities, we then must craft a gentle blending of following and leading, receiving and giving, being and doing. If we expect obedience from others, we must also learn to obey. Listening for God's instructions, furthermore, does not happen only at the beginning of a task. Obedience must flow through the midst of each day as we measure our tasks and decisions in light of God's intent and our mission and purpose.

It is a worthy goal to live on more than one level at once, to conduct our external affairs with expertise while experiencing God's grace at a deeper, internal level. Inward worship can be a constant counterpoint to events in our visible world. In this way, we do not dichotomize or split apart our experiences as persons of faith and as professionals. Instead, we can allow these two parts of our lives to work in creative tension, each enhancing and informing the other.

What happens when we listen to the voice of the soul calling? For one thing, we gain greater moral awareness, which can guide us when we are faced with difficult life choices. When we learn to listen to our inner voice, it becomes easier to hear. We do not always need a burning bush or a bolt of lightning to know that God is speaking to us. Sometimes it happens intuitively. Flora Slosson Wuellner, a UCC minister and author of several books on spirituality, offers a special prayer that is helpful in discerning what is right and wrong when she is confronted with a decision or direction for herself. She calls this the "radical prayer" and emphasizes that we should not pray it unless we mean it: "Holy Spirit, if this is right for me, let it become more firmly rooted and established in my life. If this is wrong for me, let it become less important to me, and let it be increasingly removed from my life."[2] Wuellner shares that praying this prayer helped one woman cope with a preoccupation with earning money, guided a young man who felt a strong attraction to a married woman, and helped resolve an older man's confusion about how best to spend time during retirement years. It is a way of consulting God, seeking an inner truth to guide outward behaviors.

A Quaker named Thomas Kelly described this way of life in his 1941 book *A Testament of Devotion*. He began by talking about our inner lack of integration, a condition that makes it hard to know what voice to obey:

> We are trying to be several selves at once, without all our selves being organized by a single, mastering Life within us. Each of us tends to be, not a single self, but a whole committee of selves. There is the civic self, the parental self, the financial self, the religious self, the society self, the professional self, the literary self. And each of our selves is in turn a rank individualist, not cooperative but shouting out his vote loudly for himself when the voting time comes. Often we feel divided rather than guided by one ultimate purpose. It is easiest then to settle for a "majority vote" among our committee of many selves, though this is more expedient than satisfying.[3]

Holy obedience means living from a deep Center. This Center is formed through daily habits. It is formed by intentional efforts to establish an inward worship, which is a constant counterpoint to events in our visible world. For example, one of my friends begins each day by reading one of the lectionary passages for the upcoming Sunday. He then holds the scripture text side by side with his schedule and tries to see how the biblical message might speak to each task. He prays about the meetings he will have, the people he will talk with, and the plans he will make. At a deep level, this reminds him that his life is lived with sacred purpose, and each single responsibility can add up to a significant ministry. This same discernment process can take place at the end of the day rather than the beginning. Sometimes I write down in a journal what I have done in one day and ask God to show me how my telephone calls, counseling sessions, and family time have been expressions of my faith.

Living on two levels is also the mark of a leader with foresight. This servant-leader is immersed in the real world of deadlines and events, but also remains detached enough from the details of today's tasks to see the efforts in the perspective of history or projected into the long-term future. Greenleaf points out the practical benefit in this outlook, which allows you to act constructively to forestall ethical or practical problems while you still have the freedom to change course.[4]

The reward of this holy obedience is a life lived not only with profound meaning and appreciation, but also with an overwhelming awareness of God's enveloping love. This love embraces the soul and is radiated out to persons in your care. It is no small gift.

≋ Following Jesus

Jesus embodied diakonal ministry. When he called the disciples to serve one another, he used a Greek word that is literally translated as "waiting at table." It implied a very personal service rendered to another, an act of love. This work of providing for others' needs was usually seen as women's work, and to the Greeks it was not very dignified. However, Judaism and Eastern thought saw nothing unworthy in serving, especially when one serves a great master. Jesus also expanded the concept of *diakonia* from serving at a table to providing shelter and clothing to persons in need, and visiting the sick and the prisoner. For Christ, this was part of bringing God's dominion to earth and inaugurating the age of glory. He said, "Go and tell John what you hear and see: the blind receive their sight, the lame walk, the lepers are cleansed, the deaf hear, the dead are raised, and the poor have good news brought to them" (Matt. 11:4–5).

In the Epistles of the Christian Scriptures, there is a strong message that gifts are entrusted to us so that we may serve others. The apostle Paul exhorted young congregations to gather and distribute a collection (1 Cor. 16:1–2). The work was equated with obedience to our all-powerful God. Paul realized he was asking a lot of the early Christians, but reminded them in Second Corinthians that all members of the community are mutually giving and receiving:

> I do not mean that there should be relief for others and pressure on you, but it is a question of a fair balance between your present abundance and their need, so that their abundance may be for your need, in order that there may be a fair balance. As it is written, "The one who had much did not have too much, and the one who had little did not have too little." (2 Cor. 8:13–15)

Like Jesus and the apostles, we will discover that serving God's people is often frustrating. Many of them are ungrateful and uncooperative. In the words of Greenleaf, "Anybody could lead perfect people—if there were any. But there aren't any perfect people."[5] Or as one of my friends says, "The problem with health and human services is all the humans." The challenge of Christian servanthood is to act with the love that people *deserve* even in times when they do not seem to deserve it, or to love people who cannot love you back.

As a parent of young children, I am reminded of this lesson almost daily. No experience could be more humbling. When their behavior certainly does not merit love, we are called to discipline our children while still maintaining unconditional love for them. Following through in this way requires restraint that comes naturally to very few of us! I know there are frustrating moments for me as a parent when I have to stop, take some deep breaths, and remember the peace I once felt in my daughters' more angelic moments. Doing this restores my spirit enough so that I can speak to them from my abiding love for them rather than from my anger in the moment. Then I wonder how my parents put up with me as a child, and I realize my life as a humble servant is not going to end anytime soon.

≋ Resisting Evil

To practice obedience to God, we must constantly battle the life-denying power of evil and sin. The powers of death continue to seduce us; there is no shortage of evidence for this in our experiences and the daily news. Our bewildering attachment to the "sins which cling so closely" is an essential theme in Donne's Holy Sonnet XIV from the *Divine Meditations*. He uses the image of a woman who is helplessly caught up in the forces of evil and alienation, who is surrounded by the enemies of God and cannot manage to break free. She seeks an end to this separation between her psyche and God, which will result in a form of spiritual marriage between God and her soul. Knowing that it will be difficult, she demands that God forcibly deliver her from this living death. Halfhearted efforts will not be enough to break the grip of sin upon her spirit. She describes herself as being "bethroth'd unto your enemie," the devil, and asks God to bring a powerful and intense love that will set her free:

> Yet dearely I love you, and would be lov'd faine,
> But am betroth'd unto your enemie,
> Divorce me, untie, or break that knot again,
> Take me to you, imprison me, for I
> Except you enthrall me, never shall be free,
> Nor ever chast, except you ravish mee.[6]

This theme was existentially real for Donne, who led a tumultuous life from 1572 to 1631 in England. Known as a writer of erotic verse in his younger years, he was encouraged to pursue a vocation in the ministry and eventually became a chaplain to King James I. He secretly eloped with his wife, Anne, and later they were grieved by the deaths of five of their twelve children. Plagued by doubts and tempted to pursue another kind of life, Donne applied himself to writing and preaching and gained a large popular following during his life and afterward. Through the centuries his wrestling with sexuality, spirituality, mortality, and vocation has struck a resonant chord in many other souls.

Our Puritan ancestors, contemporaries of Donne, engaged in systematic prayer and meditation centering on similar themes. They would first meditate on their need to die to sin through self-examination and confession. Then, gradually, through reading the Bible and singing psalms, they would receive a renewed experience of God's grace. Charles Hambrick-Stowe, a UCC minister and historian, describes the Puritan devotional cycle in this way: "Typically, evening devotions concentrated on preparation for death and confession of sin (for one might not wake up), placing oneself in God's eternal hands. Morning devotions tended to be resurrection-centered, full of thanksgiving." Spiritual diaries of Puritans such as Anne Bradstreet and Edward Taylor record the "resurrection" experiences of ecstatic union with Christ using the language of sexuality, as Donne did. How else could they describe this experience of intense and intimate reconciliation, Hambrick-Stowe asks.[7]

As a lover of the Hebrew Scriptures, I sometimes turn to Deuteronomy for guidance about good and evil. This book contains thirty-four chapters of laws and preaching concerning rules of right conduct, on every subject from marriage to food to farming to worship. But for me, it is all summarized in a sermon given by Moses when he was 120 years old:

> See, I have set before you today life and prosperity, death and adversity. If you obey the commandments of the Sovereign God that I am commanding you today, by loving the Sovereign God, walking in God's ways, and observing divine commandments, decrees, and ordinances, then you shall live and become numerous, and the Sovereign God will bless you in the land that you are entering to possess. But if your heart turns away and you do not hear, but are led astray to bow down to other gods and serve them, I declare to you today that you shall perish; you shall not live long in the land that you are crossing the Jordan to enter and possess. I call heaven and earth to witness against you today

that I have set before you life and death, blessings and curses.
Choose life so that you and your descendants may live, loving
the Sovereign God, obeying God, and holding fast to God; for
that means life to you and length of days. (Deut. 30:15–20)

We are all given the choice to make between pursuing the path
that leads to life or following the one that leads to death. Many of
us experience a kind of death in life; I am deeply troubled by persons who seem to intentionally *choose* to engage in habits and out-
looks that lead to misery when life-affirming possibilities are available to them. God holds out life to us in every moment, including
the bleakest hours of our existence. The alternatives are set before
us with radical freedom—to choose God's love and life abundant,
even in the midst of ambiguity.

≋ Moving Forward after Pain

I often turn to a poem that speaks to me of the power derived
through age and experience. As we submit, often unwillingly, again
and again to God's intentions for us, we may feel that our lives and
our selves are not turning out as we would have wished. But if we
are able to accept the mantle of servanthood and the humbling
lessons that accompany it, and if we are able to live in harmony
with our spiritual nature, there is also incredible strength that
comes with time. The poem is "The Sycamore," by Wendell Berry:

> In the place that is my own place, whose earth
> I am shaped in and must bear, there is an old tree growing,
> a great sycamore that is a wondrous healer of itself.
> Fences have been tied to it, nails driven into it,
> hacks and whittles cut in it, the lightning has burned it.
> There is no year it has flourished in
> that has not harmed it. There is a hollow in it
> that is its death, though its living brims whitely

at the lip of the darkness and flows outward.
Over all its scars has come the seamless white
of the bark. It bears the gnarls of its history
healed over. It has risen to a strange perfection
in the warp and bending of its long growth.
It has gathered all accidents into its purpose.
It has become the intention and radiance of its dark fate.
It is a fact, sublime, mystical and unassailable.
In all the country there is no other like it.
I recognize in it a principle, an indwelling
the same as itself, and greater, that I would be ruled by.
I see that it stands in its place, and feeds upon it,
and is fed upon, and is native, and maker.[8]

I resonate with the beauty of Berry's images of the damaged and yet triumphant tree, and its feeding upon and providing for the life that surrounds it. Wendell Berry is a Kentucky farmer who also writes novels, poems, and essays. For me, the sycamore tree represents the image of the Christian servant and his or her interrelationship with God. We are the offspring of Holiness, part of the sacred image, and yet also co-creators with God in overflowing and eternal love. We have been wounded and have received the balm of grace. We have suffered and yet experienced salvation. I am reminded of a quotation from Joseph Campbell: "Like a candle in a holy place is the beauty of the aged face." The wrinkles and lines etched by years of living do not make us less attractive, but are signs of our ability to survive.

Perhaps all of us know someone who lives on "borrowed time." Such people are living testimonies to holy obedience, for they know there is no reason for them still to walk this earth. Wilbur, in his early seventies, accepted his doctor's prognosis that he had only a few months to live. He sold his house and came to the nursing home with his cancer and his books, and told me when he arrived, "I came here to die and I'm happy about that." A devoted Christian, Wilbur at first spent his days lying in bed, waiting for the cancer to eat away at his vital signs and take him to heaven. But death was not quite ready for Wilbur, and he started feeling better after several days. He couldn't resist his natural inclination to socialize; share books, magazines, and even videos with the other residents; join in the Bible study; attend worship; critique the sermons; and register for a college class! Wilbur ended up becoming one of the most beloved residents in the nursing home, known by everyone, and lived another three years. He made the most of time, and was very much alive in his dying. Wilbur accepted these years as a wonderful surprise.

Donne's plea that God "break, blow, burn" the barriers that separate the soul from God clearly acknowledges that this process can bring pain as well as blessing. Yet the goal is ultimately purification, as Bianco da Siena expressed in the words to the hymn "Come Forth, O Love Divine," originally written in 1367:

> O Comforter, draw near,
> Within my heart appear,
> And kindle it, Thy holy flame bestowing.
> O let it freely burn,
> Till earthly passions turn
> To dust and ashes in its heat consuming.[9]

Greenleaf has some excellent words about the spiritual wisdom that can be derived from loss and change. He writes about it in the essay "An Inward Journey" reflecting upon a Robert Frost poem called "Directive":

> To be on with the journey one must have an attitude toward loss and being lost, a view of oneself in which powerful symbols like *burned, dissolved, broken off*—however painful their impact is seen to be—do not appear as senseless or destructive. Rather the losses they suggest are seen as opening the way for new creative acts, for the receiving of priceless gifts. Loss, *every loss one's*

mind can conceive of, creates a vacuum into which will come (if allowed) something new and fresh and beautiful, something unforeseen—and the greatest of these is *love.*[10]

A deeply felt loss may hurt us, but it can also teach us to share our pain and vulnerability with others in an honest, human way. I will always remember a comment made by one of our nursing home residents following a chapel service I had conducted. "I enjoy listening to you so much," she said, "because your voice just sounds like you're in love with all of us!" There is something about the act of worship, both inward worship and corporate worship, that brings me to a profound awareness of the depths of God's love for me and for all of us. This serenity that we can know within ourselves is a gift of peace, but it reaches fulfillment when it is shared in community with kindred spirits.

≋ 6

Learning Interdependence
in a World of Autonomy

And make me new.
                —John Donne

Servants feel we must be strong for others. Taking on problems such as AIDS, homelessness, marital conflict, child abuse, and health care reform is not for the faint of heart. We feel we need to be strong so that others can lean upon us and depend upon us. What is that strength? What does it mean to be strong?

≋ Strength

Strength can be claimed by acknowledging our weakness and learning to depend upon others. It is too easy for Christian servants to slip into the old stereotype of being "lonely at the top," which can lead to abuse of power, errors of judgment, and rigid thinking. An excellent example is the story of King David of Israel, who desired Bathsheba and saw to it that her husband, Uriah the Hittite, was killed in battle so that David could marry the beautiful woman. After that terrible lapse, God sent the prophet Nathan to speak to David, confronting him with his sin by telling a morality tale that actually described David's situation (2 Sam. 12:1–25). When David recognized he was guilty of the same sin described in Nathan's parable, he was moved to repentance. Even the most powerful need courageous people to correct them and keep them accountable. Loneliness can also be destructive when our doubts and concern turn inward to self-flagellation. Many contemporary writers encourage servant-leaders to see themselves as being first among equals or as serving with a group or team rather than at the top of the hierarchy.

Strength also comes from being able to confront our inner spiritual deficits and vulnerabilities. Strength comes not from holding God (and other people) at a distance, but from allowing God to break and burn the rotting timbers in the structures of the soul so that we might be made new. It will bring us into suffering and through the pain of sorrow, but we will rise again through the strength of God's Spirit. Strength leads us through the heart, in the path of powerlessness. The apostle Paul described his limitations in the second letter to the Corinthians. Paul's famous "thorn in the flesh" tormented him but also kept him from "being too elated":

> Three times I appealed to God about this, that it would leave me, but God said to me, "My grace is sufficient for you, for power is made perfect in weakness." So, I will boast all the more gladly of my weaknesses, so that the power of Christ may dwell in me. Therefore I am content with weaknesses, insults, hardships, persecutions, and calamities for the sake of Christ; for whenever I am weak, then I am strong. (2 Cor. 12:8–10)

It is a profound truth of Christian faith that we must admit our failings and thorns in the flesh before we can find the strength to overcome them. I have been very encouraged to see that more Protestant congregations are willing to come to terms with the needs of their members through healing services and services of reconciliation. In these very moving worship experiences, individuals seek the support and prayers of the congregation as they openly admit their need for healing from a spiritual, physical, or emotional wound. We need to turn more often to our brothers and sisters in faith in these times rather than seek help only from a medical doctor or therapist. There is a power in spiritual community that cannot be duplicated.

I think of the couple with one nondisabled three-year-old son whose second child was born with Down's syndrome. Not knowing about the new baby's condition before his birth, the family members were thrown into chaos as they tried to adjust to his needs. Members of their suburban church came to the rescue and provided volunteers every day for several hours to help the new mother, the baby, and his older sibling. This support continued until the child was one year old, and ever since then the boy has been "adopted" as a favored child of the congregation.

Not all of us have learned to depend upon other people for support in this way. Flora Slosson Wuellner offers some knowing insights into the contemporary problems of Christian servant-leaders who assume too much responsibility for their lives and work without relying on the strength of others in their community:

> One of the main causes of leadership fatigue is our temptation to feel that it's all up to us. This is the problem of super-responsibility. We feel that God's kingdom stands or falls according to the extent of our willpower, our righteous efficiency, and our power to love and heal. Perhaps we have learned to delegate responsibility outwardly, but we have not learned it inwardly. We carry the burdens of all upon our hearts and never take an inner vacation. We overlook Jesus' challenge to be the branches of the vine (John 15:4–5) and try to become the vine ourselves. Without realizing what has happened, we are trying to become the generators rather than the transmitters of divine energy.[1]

She goes on to describe the signs of inner fatigue: anxiety and nervousness, absentmindedness, annoyance over trifles, exasperation at other people, unrestful sleep, loss of joy, a feeling of being driven or constrained. These symptoms may be a result of being too autonomous and placing too many expectations upon ourselves in a life of service.

Sometimes we have to bottom out, or reach a crisis point, before we are able to call upon the resources of our community for strength. A fascinating example comes from the book *Turning Stones: My Days and Nights with Children at Risk*. Author Marc Parent describes his job for three years as a social worker in New York City. He responded to emergency calls on nights and weekends that came from people reporting parents who were abusing or neglecting their children. As the months passed, the shock value of the home visits he made gradually wore him down. After one terrible case in which an infant died from malnutrition, Parent finally reached the point where he knew he had lost his ability to effectively judge whether it was better to pull a child out of a home or leave the child in a familiar, though potentially dangerous, situation. When he took time off to cope with the horror of his misjudgment and its fatal result, he suddenly remembered an experience from his childhood in Wisconsin. It was a story with religious meaning, and it became a healing and hopeful memory for him.

One day a nun who taught in Parent's private elementary school shared with the class a story from her summer vacation. While visiting Death Valley on a bus trip to the American West with other nuns, she was impressed by the awesome power and immensity of the stones that filled the landscape. Before she left the site, she felt moved to flip over one of the rocks, simply as a sign that she had been there. At first, the other sisters were skeptical, but as the trip continued, all of the nuns were turning stones at every stop along the way. They all wanted to feel a part of this notable history, and turning stones was a way to ensure that these beautiful places were just a little bit different because each of them had been there. This phrase has a dual meaning: turning stones is a physical feat that causes a change in the landscape, but it also refers metaphorically to the spirit of exploration and mystery ("leaving no stone unturned").

Recalling this story enabled Parent to reenvision his efforts in child welfare. Instead of succumbing to despair and apathy, he went back to work knowing that although he could not deliver all children from pain, he could be the one to turn a stone in the lives of a few children. And his involvement would make a difference to them.[2]

Strength is not for each of us alone. While the inner journey is worthy of dignity and privacy, there are ways of sharing it in community, *koinonia,* the gathering of the faithful. God will lead us to companions, to friends for the soul who come from unexpected places. Our hearts are stretched, in joy and pain, yet we are led through the very heart of God and emerge with a truer knowledge of others. It is a very powerful thing when, after offering a prayer or compassionate words to someone in need, that person then offers to say a prayer for *you.* This is the value of community, knowing that those who are serving have an equal need to *be served.*

Servanthood by its definition is exercised in community, which is a form of discipline for those of us raised to "do our own thing." Jesus stressed that no one was greater than anyone else, and that members of the Christian community must be interdependent: "The greatest among you must become like the youngest, and the leader like one who serves. For who is greater, the one who is at the table or the one who serves? Is it not the one at the table? But I am among you as one who serves" (Luke 22:26–27). Participation in community requires compromise, openness, and a willingness to be vulnerable. Spiritual friends give us the courage to confront our inner deficits, to gain new insights, and to offer the same in return. Community also allows us to join together in rituals of celebration, mourning, and gratitude, granting us a sense of belonging and inviting other servants to acknowledge God's presence in our daily routine.

Community is a form of spiritual discipline, and like any other, it does not happen by itself. Although technology has in many ways made the world smaller, it has also made neighbors strangers and strangers neighbors. How often I have taken a walk in my neighborhood on a beautiful day and have seen almost no one outdoors because in most cases they are huddled inside, around the glow of the television or computer screen. In addition, the information overload of our media-saturated culture has led to what many call "compassion fatigue." As people are exposed to more and more violence and tragedy, caring about any of it becomes harder.

On the other hand, the nature of community has changed radically, so that now we can be physically, emotionally, and sometimes spiritually dependent upon those who are far from us. For instance, an eleven-year-old boy in the Midwest was participating in a chat room on the Internet when he got an urgent message for medical help from another person who was also on-line at the time. It turned out that his computer correspondent was a young woman in New Zealand who was experiencing difficulty breathing and did not have the strength to get up from her chair. Using the telephone and computer lines, the boy was able to notify paramedics on another continent, and they were able to save the young woman's life! Along with its obvious dangers and limitations, technology clearly offers new possibilities for community.

Community must be sought, maintained, and redefined—whether it is in the workplace, in the home, by telephone, or in a prayer chapel on the World Wide Web. The potential for losing meaningful relationships has increased greatly in our times. Spiritual friends come and go, communal feeling may be fleeting, and sometimes we feel the effort is not worthwhile. But we cannot give up, because community is as necessary for spiritual life as is individual meditation. There are ways of knowing God that can be experienced only in the company of others, and God desires to be known by us in fullness. Community is an essential element of spiritual transformation.

Here, too, the Congregationalists offer a model of spiritual community. It was common for each family to engage in daily devotions, and each family was considered a church. Christians shared in private conferences to watch over the spiritual welfare of their neighbors. They engaged in "godly conversation" with one another, and their reading of the Bible had true life and meaning for the early Americans. They often shared Scripture passages that they felt had a direct impact on the situation they were encountering together. Spiritual friendships and family worship not only lifted the soul into closer relationship with Christ, but also renewed the individual for Christian service. Farmers, housewives, ministers, and merchants supported one another and the community in con-templative practices that led to social action.

In contrast, many Christians today are so afraid of saying the wrong thing about God or faith, we often don't say anything at all. We observe an unspoken spiritual privatism. How do we find a meaningful spiritual community today? Where can we experience a sense of belonging, a place where we feel safe and accepted, where we can share our secrets and be privileged to listen to the soul voices of others? A place where we do not feel controlled or stifled but where we can begin to articulate what seems inexpressible? Is it possible to draw upon the resources of institutional soul?

≋ Forms of Community

In the excellent article "The Community of Faith" published in 1997 by the United Church Board for Homeland Ministries, Dr. J. Mary Luti explores the various uses of the word "community." It may define a group of people in the same geographic location, peo-ple who share a common endeavor, or people who share Christian beliefs and practices; or it may refer to a somewhat romantic ideal of human solidarity. She goes on to describe ways in which com-munities can be central to living a disciplined Christian life. A group of committed Christian persons may develop into a commu-nity intentionally or spontaneously, but they will not exist primar-ily for therapy or adult education, she says:

> Rather, they are meant for discernment and support in accepting more and more fully the invitation of the gospel to abundant life. Help is available in them for personal devotion, the growth of Christian character, civic responsibility, work, family, and the many ways we are engaged in loving our neighbor and announc-ing the good news to the poor. Naming, confessing, and resisting evil and the continual offer of forgiveness may also be crucial components of their mutual ministry.[3]

The gifts of participating in spiritual community include commitment; perseverance; a wider horizon; a sense of the real; and shared witness. Luti comments, "That a group of believers should meet, share faith, and help each other's life with God to grow is a powerful form of evangelism. Despite its inevitable flaws and spectacular failures, community remains a living gospel, a privileged angle on *shalom*, a compelling witness to the world."[4]

On the other hand, Luti admits, there are obstacles to creating community. We fear what will happen if we commit ourselves to walking with others, or we feel uncomfortable sharing our faith in an intimate way. We are afraid of disapproval from others, being labeled or misjudged by others inside or outside the community. We also lack time, which is required for a supportive community to grow and bear fruit. Some of us simply may not know how to go about the task of creating community.

Groups that may become communities include the following:

— volunteer groups
— support groups for persons living with the same problem or addiction
— groups of persons who share similar work or life situations, e.g., young mothers, retirees, clergy, college students
— neighborhood Bible study groups
— small discipleship groups within churches
— gender-specific groups, e.g., men's or women's spirituality retreats
— groups that agree to pray together, for and with one another
— groups that gather for spiritual direction
— athletic teams and exercise partners
— lovers of the arts and humanities who seek meaning through creative expression
— Internet chat rooms and e-mail subscribers
— civic and service organizations
— advocacy groups for programs such as Habitat for Humanity and Amnesty International

Finding the elusive community does not always mean starting something new. Sometimes we are already members of a community, and all we need to do is to recover the *spiritual* intent, meaning, and purpose of the group to which we already belong. This may happen in a marriage, a family, a neighborhood, a workplace, a social group, or among friends. The sense of community, in turn, will inspire in its members trust, respect, and ethical behavior toward others, according to Robert Greenleaf. He says, "Living in community as one's basic involvement will generate an exportable surplus of love which the individual may carry into his many involvements with institutions which are usually not communities: businesses, churches, governments, schools."[5] These communities can arise within institutions, which are not natural communities, when servant-leaders show the way by demonstrating their love and sense of responsibility for a specific group of individuals. Another mark of a true community is that it is people building rather than people using. People who belong to the community are not merely a means to a greater end; they are in themselves worthy, valuable, and God's beloved children.

It is natural for us to need the inspiration and support of others to know how best to live, and it is particularly true in the life of faith that we need to be fed by the experience of others—both living and dead. One person who tries to carry the leadership of a community alone will often find creativity destroyed, judgment skewed, and energies sapped. We rely upon the inspiration of others who have gone before us. As Reinhold Niebuhr observed:

> The average man does not live so dynamically, and the springs of life do not flow so purely in him, that he is able to maintain a wholesome attitude toward life without leaning a little on spiritual resources created by other more dynamic and more vigorous persons. If this attempt to borrow strength from others, which is the very basis of all institutional religion, does not tempt us to cease from all effort of our own, it can be a source of real moral power.[6]

≋ New Communities

Clearly, there are times when communities evolve naturally. In other contexts, community must be created or re-created. In the helpful essay "Spirited Connections: Learning to Tap the Spiritual Resources in Our Lives and Work," D. Susan Wisely and Elizabeth M. Lynn suggest several ideas for building community.[7]

First, they suggest that conversation, particularly in the form of storytelling, is helpful in creating personal and communal connections. Questions to ask may include: Where did you go to elementary school? What were the most important lessons your parents taught you? Who was your best friend when you were a teenager? What was your first job and how did you get it? Where and when were you baptized? How do you have fun? If you were going to write the story of your life, what would you call it? If your life story were made into a movie, who would play the lead? Depending upon the trust level of the group, you may ask more serious questions. A leader who may seem aloof and arrogant is quickly brought down to earth when she tells her staff that she grew up raising chickens or growing cucumbers on the family farm. We are much more easily motivated by a person's humanity than by professional competence. In retreat settings, it is meaningful to ask people to bring with them a "sacred object." It may be a photograph, a piece of jewelry, or a memento that reminds them of something precious. Sharing and explaining the sacred objects in the group can build a sense of community.

Second, building community means taking time to consider the group's mission and vision. This should not happen in a forced, top-down fashion, but through the process of emergence from the grassroots. The community then must commit to staying accountable to the common vision and responding to challenges. For instance, if an organization claims to value its employees and includes this commitment in its vision statement, what happens when there are layoffs or downsizing? Is the vision quickly dismissed as "pie in the sky," or can it be reexamined? Are there ways the organization can still value the staff when there are cutbacks? How can communication happen so that people are involved in making decisions that will affect them, so that the community then shares responsibility for both positive and negative consequences of change?

Third, Wisely and Lynn suggest examining the story or history of the community. How does our current story fit in the context of the larger story? How is each member of the group a part of the emerging history of the community? Recently, in the process of developing a policy and procedure book for the pastoral care department, the director decided to include a historical page recording the names of chaplains at Lifelink over the last century. It placed the whole document in a different context, reminding current staff that someday their work might also be recorded and become part of the history of ministry in our organization.

Fourth, the authors suggest community is formed by the old-fashioned custom of reading together. Taking time to read and discuss the same books or articles forms a moral community, a community of reflection, a community where ideas are respected and discussed. Interacting with particular books from our separate perspectives defines ways in which our individual stories are separate and one. We gain new understandings and appreciations for other members of our community, and we are also connected to knowledge and information from the wider world.

Many people find community in twelve-step programs focused on overcoming addiction. These communities are powerful because they draw on the support of others with a common problem (the horizontal dimension of support) and on the help of God or a higher power (the vertical dimension). But twelve-step groups are also limited as a primary source of spiritual community because participants are known to one another fundamentally as persons coping with addiction rather than in a holistic way. Still, the honesty and mutuality of twelve-step programs have led to deep spiritual and personal growth for thousands of people, and they demonstrate the transformational potential of any community.

≋ Time Apart

In this chapter on autonomy and interdependence we cannot overlook the fact that solitude and silence also need to be respected in community. The rhythm of engagement and retreat actually allows the whole body to grow, and sometimes the best thing we can do for community is to allow separateness. Each member of a community is responsible to live his or her own life, to cultivate personal interests and self-nurture, and not to expect the group to supply all needs.

We are called by Christ to move back and forth between solitude and community, as he did. When we withdraw into our own privacy, it is not *from* community but *to* community in a different form. For instance, within a family each member needs time alone and time with others. We can be very present to one another in times when we are physically separated, and we can also observe silence or allow for distance between us when we are together in the same place. Learning to be alone without feeling lonely can make us better companions for others.

As members of one body, we need to function effectively, but we must always remain cognizant of our debts and obligations to the rest of the body. They give us reason to celebrate. We can breathe spirit into our lives of service through healthy partnerships in community. Brian O. McDermott offers effective closing words in an essay titled "Partnering with God":

> God wants to act in, through, and with groups of human beings, provided they are intent on the flourishing of human beings and not on their harm or destruction. Partnering with God, finding one's deepest identity in one's relationship with God, and developing a sense of God's longing to act in and with groups can help a person . . . stay in the fray for the long haul.[8]

≈ **7**

Bringing Spirituality
into a Life of Service

Theology is not a provable accumulation, like
science, nor is it a succession of enduring
moments, like art. It must always unravel and
be reknit.

—*John Updike*, Hugging the Shore

I sit on two ethics committees that discuss issues of professional
practice in services to children and older people. We have debated
cases ranging from whether to terminate life-supporting treatment
for a comatose person to whether we should halt an adoption
because the potential adoptive mother had just been diagnosed
with end-stage cancer. As we examine the competing ethical values
involved, I often think that each committee member's opinions
reflect private belief systems. This is an extremely valuable and rare
experience: to be able to connect personal piety with public life in a
secure and respectful environment. I wish more people could have
this experience.

As theology needs forever to be "reknit," so outward action
needs to be "knit together" with the inner voice of the soul. When
we do not or cannot listen to the soul calling, our lives unravel, and
we begin to feel detached and alienated from the service we provide. In this final chapter, I suggest ways to connect the life of spirituality *and* service through rituals and spiritual practices.

≋ Ritual

Our spirits come alive most of all through ritual, an area of life that has become impoverished in an increasingly secular culture. Rituals are corporate acts that define and sustain our souls and the souls of our communities. What are our rituals in diakonal ministry? What rituals do we need? What are the ways that we ritualize new beginnings and ceremonialize endings in a way that points beyond the immediate present?

Rituals feed our souls by providing symbolic events that dramatize in a visible way what is unseen within and beyond us, making us more conscious of the power of the spiritual world. Rituals, when they are sensitively constructed and authentically celebrated, give us a feeling of belonging, a kinship, a sense that we have at last found a home in this lonely world. Without rituals, we devalue our elders, overlook our children, and leave our adults bewildered and confused. Rituals invite God to help us.

Rituals are powerful because they touch us at the sensory, emotional level, they make use of repetition to connect us with our spirituality, and they use symbols to express intangible realities. Candles, incense, or an old favorite hymn can instantly evoke long-forgotten memories and emotions. Words of the Rosary or the Latin Mass or the Twenty-third Psalm are almost instinctive for people who grew up with those traditions. As Peg Thompson observed: "In a way that nothing else can, rituals place our lives in a sacred context. Through our rituals, we discover and rediscover sustaining images for the life of our spirit, and we affirm the core values of our spiritual life."[1]

Though we have a deep need for meaningful rituals, rote prayers and routines are often the limit of spiritual life experienced by individuals and groups. While it is good to share a common tradition, it is also dangerous if we never vary the way our tradition is used and we lose a sense of the true meaning of the ritual. For instance, one church I know has a tradition of reciting the Prayer of Jesus at the close of church meetings. The people would be much better served to recite phrases from the prayer *during* their deliberations rather than use it in closing as a kind of blessing for whatever has gone before. Routines can compartmentalize religious faith, making spirituality separate from the rest of life rather than allowing it to flow naturally through life's center.

We need to develop rituals that can be used in sacred and secular settings (or that transform secular environments into sacred spaces), that make real for people the knowledge that they are indeed part of the blessed community. The word "liturgy," which we use to describe the order of service used by a community of faith, literally means the "work of the people." We may invite members of our communities to participate in rituals that uncover the spiritual presence in our common work. Rituals should be designed to respond to the needs of the community, such as having a blessing service for a new bus to transport community members; dedicating a new building, program, mural, or piece of artwork; conducting a blessing service for animals and pets; commissioning a new volunteer for service; blessing newly adopted children in a family; recognizing the divorce of two valued community members; and celebrating a renewal of vows for couples who have been married more than fifty years. Such creative rituals can be taken too far and should be designed with discretion. But we all hunger for rituals, even events as commonplace as birthday parties, that make us feel we are significant members of the community.

Also, there are simple, individual rituals—ways to practice silence, pause for prayer, and express gratitude and petition in ordinary life. These small habits can bring us closer to God as we go about serving others. Sometimes we must give up things that distract us from devotion to service. At other times we need to engage in practices that unveil what is occurring on the spiritual level in our daily lives. To do this most effectively, you should identify your spiritual style, the spiritual experiences that best suit your religious temperament. For some, repeating memorized prayers or phrases is very helpful. For others, doing that is boring, and spontaneous prayers are much more meaningful. You may wish to explore a book called *Prayer and Temperament* for a more detailed description of how to identify your prayer type.[2]

≈ Spiritual Practices

Here are some suggestions that may breathe spirit into your life of service.

Keep a Bible in your workplace or in a prominent place in your home. It is a reminder to you and others that spirituality is part of your daily life, not something reserved only for special occasions.

Read from a devotional book every day. This habit takes only a few minutes, but I find it is one of the most important parts of my day. There are hundreds of daily devotional books written for persons from all walks of life, available in religious and nonreligious bookstores or through catalog or Web site booksellers. Some are denominational; others are ecumenical. Make this your inspirational time, whether it is in the morning, afternoon, evening, or middle of the night.

Read and share prayers. If you need some fresh ideas for expressing your prayers, find a collection written by someone else. Oxford publishes some excellent compilations of prayers written by people from a wide variety of backgrounds. Or you may enjoy a more lighthearted collection. If a prayer makes you think of someone special, send it to that person. Write down prayers or quotations you like, and keep them on an index card in your wallet. You never know when you may need to glance at them. Many classic prayers are available on cards or bookmarks in gift shops.

Read and discuss poetry, articles, and books with other people. When I speak or preach, people are very appreciative of brief synopses or quotations from good literature. Perhaps because visual media tend to dominate our lives, many people feel they do not have enough time for reading and writing. It is more common to discuss a movie or television show that everyone has seen rather than a compelling book that everyone has read. Taking time to thoughtfully discuss ideas presented in written form reminds us to slow down, to listen to one another, and to hear the calling of our souls.

Form a prayer group or spiritual formation group. It may have two members or twenty. A useful resource is *A Spiritual Formation Workbook* by James Bryan Smith.[3] (See chapter 6 on community for more ideas.)

Keep a journal. Some people consider this spiritual discipline tedious, but others love it. Journals of all types are available in bookstores, from blank books to spiral-bound notebooks with space for daily jottings (such as *In Good Company* published by United Church Press). I recommend that everyone journal occasionally, particularly in times of transition or loss. Many people find it helpful to write letters to loved ones who have died, or to work out concerns about a relationship in a letter that is never sent. Some people like to journal about their dreams, their prayer life, or their progress in attaining a certain goal. It should not be something that will make you feel guilty if you do not do it for a while. Don't force it, but if this is a natural medium for you, it will be very productive.

Meditate. Many books are available on meditation, some Christian, some from other religious traditions, some secular. Common recommendations are that you meditate in the same place and at the same time every day and that you focus on your breathing as a means of putting aside distractions and concentrating on spiritual awareness. My somewhat unorthodox advice is that you can also meditate while performing a mindless task such as stuffing envelopes or while you are waiting in line. We don't always have the luxury of predictability in modern life, so I believe in taking advantage of opportunities for spiritual time whenever they come along.

Reserve a time of silence in each day (while driving, while falling asleep, while waking up, etc.) when you allow your thoughts and prayers to freely drift through your consciousness. You may wish to talk to God out loud, to think about people on your prayer list, or not to have any agenda at all during this quiet time.

Read theology or devotional classics. It is especially helpful to read an author from an unfamiliar tradition or background. If you find a writer who seems to speak to you, keep reading his or her books. Many of the great spiritual writings have come from Catholic authors, but Protestants are beginning to get more shelf space. My soul seems to resonate most with writers from the Quaker tradition.

Don't forget to laugh. It is hard for me to keep a straight face when I see people in a sanctuary reciting, "Let us rejoice," in mournful, solemn monotones. Although religion is a very serious matter, our God obviously has a sense of humor. When we laugh, we should express joy in living, not scorn. Laughter is a form of spiritual wisdom, accepting that while everything in life is not as we would wish it to be, we can still live into the future with hope— giving thanks for what is good. Humor can be a healing force.

Spend time with children and older people. Separating the generations, or neglecting one at the expense of another, is unnatural and unspiritual. We need to take seriously people at different stages in life, allowing the blunt questions of a child or the bitter despair of an older adult to challenge and inform us.

Hold a "Blessing of the Hands" service for people who serve others, such as nurses, doctors, therapists, and/or caregivers. Honor the sacred work of healing, teaching, leading, or serving through a service of blessing and commissioning. These services include prayers, Scripture readings, and anointing the hands with oil that has been blessed. Another alternative is the laying on of hands to confer a blessing by touching a person's head or shoulders. A variation is to have a hand-washing ceremony. This idea comes from the story of Jesus washing the disciples' feet at the Last Supper. Although foot washing would be embarrassing and inconvenient in many modern cultures, washing the hands of other people with a basin and towel can be more easily arranged and carries the same meaning. After reading selected verses from John 13, participants pass the basin and towel and wash their neighbors' hands as an act of loving service. Or leaders may bring the basin and towel to persons individually and wash their hands one at a time.

Include prayer or time for silent discernment in meetings. This is a practice of the Shalem Institute in Bethesda, Maryland, where meetings include pauses for prayer at important decision times. It is remarkable to see what ideas will emerge when the Spirit is given a little time to work.

Allow time for open expression of grief. When a coworker has experienced the death of a friend or family member, don't expect him or her to hide sadness. Acknowledge that the individual will begin a time of mourning, and don't try to avoid mentioning the subject. People in grief need to be taken seriously, not ignored. Words of compassion and sympathy notes, even weeks after a death, are extremely important. If a member of your community has died, be sure that people know about it and have the opportunity to attend a memorial or funeral service. Honoring the memory of one who has died is a way of confronting the fact that life will no longer be the same while also giving thanks for the contributions of the person who will be missed.

Make retirements or leave-takings opportunities for ritual reminiscing and recognition, providing closure. When you know that someone will be moving to another place or position, be sure that the move is celebrated. Ask for testimonials, again acknowledging the spiritual gifts offered by that person during the time spent in your community. Bring music, photographs, and funny stories to share.

Gather in groups to discuss each individual's personal mission statement and how that is linked to the organization's or group's mission. Give people the opportunity to "rehearse" their sense of calling, to recognize and honor the gifts they started with and the progress they have made during their time of service. This is a way of reducing the sense of "us" and "them" that often occurs in organizations. There can be no community without the commitment of each person to the mission of the whole.

Talk about your spirituality. Be selective about the occasion, be sure you are not bragging or being self-righteous in the way you do this, but don't keep it a secret. For instance, if you came to an important decision as a result of prayer, tell someone. Share a thought from a sermon or devotional reading that made an impression upon you. Offer to pray for someone, and then follow up on the request. I love asking people what experiences make them feel spiritually alive. One woman admitted she feels it is a holy moment when she feeds the birds in her backyard. Another man programmed his watch to beep once every hour and used that as a reminder to say a short centering prayer. For many people I know, walking, jogging, or gardening has become their spiritual time. Sharing a simple habit you use to place God at the center of your life may truly help another person.

Go on a retreat. Clearly, Jesus practiced a form of retreat when he withdrew from the crowds in order to pray (Matt. 4:1–11; Luke 5:16; 9:28; 22:41). The danger of a retreat is that everything seems okay when we are away from daily life—then we are disappointed to return to the same old thing again. Instead, a time of retreat is designed to have meaning in and of itself, with the secondary benefit of allowing us to return home with a clearer focus. The object "is not to find God somewhere else and bring God back into the here and now, but to see the God we thought was only out there is already 'in here' and it is our dimness of vision or sin that kept us from such awareness."[4] Engaging in times of retreat allows for discernment and a fresh perspective, and provides a rhythm to our spiritual lives. Guided or preached retreats lasting two hours to several days in length are offered at many religious retreat centers. Most also allow individuals to come for private retreats, and groups can often lead their own retreat programs.

Stop at various points during the day, and say a brief prayer or pause to center your spirit. Think of God's presence during your morning shower or as you dress for the day. Take a break before a stressful task to ask God to be with you. As you meet with people or talk with them on the phone, visualize the light of God surrounding each one. When you see something beautiful, give thanks for it.[5] These incarnational spiritual practices were central in the Evangelical and Reformed tradition in the United Church of Christ.

Cultivate an attitude of gratitude. First Thessalonians 5:16–18 tells us: "Rejoice always, pray without ceasing, give thanks in all circumstances; for this is the will of God in Christ Jesus for you. Do not quench the Spirit." If we cannot think of things to be grateful for in life, we have quenched the Spirit, and we need to bring it back. Gratitude, belonging, and obedience are the fundamental tenets of Reformed spirituality. "We belong to God," begins the Heidelberg Catechism, and that in itself is always a reason to give thanks.

Stop worrying—at least for a little while. Jesus frankly could not see why we should worry about tomorrow, and he advised us to let the day's worries be sufficient for the day. Anxiety may be a sign that we believe *we* are in the driver's seat. Learn to surrender.

Keep an icon or a faith symbol nearby as a reminder of God's presence. Some people have a place to display such a sacred object or image; others carry a cross in their pocket; some people are inspired by religious calendars or computer screen-savers; some people are able to wear jewelry with a religious motif. Images of faith are more important than we think in shaping our reality and creating a Spirit-filled environment.

Surround yourself with beauty, inspiring artwork, children's pictures, and photographs of loved ones. Be connected to nature and natural objects. Nothing is more restorative to the soul, especially in times when the events in life are far from beautiful.

Mentor someone. Find a mentor for yourself. Mentoring another person helps us remember how we felt as we began our current work. Finding a mentor leads us to explore our growing edges, which leads to renewal.

Be a prophetic voice. Reframe concerns in the perspective of gospel spirituality rather than worldly values.

Slow down. Take the long view. Get a new perspective and see if you still feel the same about your situation.

Examine significant choices with spiritual discernment. Doing this should reduce your feelings of being "torn" between various alternatives. Don't do things that feel wrong to you. Ask the advice of a trusted friend when you are making an important decision.

Listen to your body and take it seriously. God speaks to us just as much through our bodies as through a "still, small voice." If you are achy or tired, there is a reason.

Allow room for spontaneity and play. You don't have to be a responsible adult all the time.

Stop during your daily routine sometimes and take a "soul check." Ask yourself, How am I feeling right now? Do I feel uncomfortable? Left out? Threatened? Angry? Am I feeling at ease and relaxed? Answering these questions helps to develop spiritual self-awareness and points toward areas of spiritual need.[6]

Accept that darkness, silence, and suffering are parts of every life, and don't overreact when these times come to you.

Visit churches other than your own. Discover what is similar and what is different. Get to know well someone from a different religious tradition. Take seriously the lessons you learn from that person.

Seek out a spiritual friend, companion, or director who will help you discover new learning and support you in your faith journey. You can locate trained spiritual directors through the Shalem Institute, seminaries and churches that have spiritual life programs, religious retreat centers, or denominational offices.

Contemplate a stained glass window or an impressive example of church architecture. Reflect on the devotion of the artisans who created it and the faith of the people who commissioned and paid for it. How does it direct you to the sacred presence in this place and time?

Celebrate. Give thanks with others when a loved one is healed, a prayer is answered, a mission is accomplished. This reminds us that the Spirit *is* at work in the world.

≋ Conclusion

As secular values flourish in our society, spiritual values may be lost or pushed aside. It is important for us as Christian servants to claim and honor the needs of our souls and to lift up the spiritual needs of the communities we serve. God grants us the means for sustaining our spirits through:

- opening our hearts to the suffering of our brothers and sisters
- acknowledging God's presence and power
- reexamining our motives and purposes in servanthood
- practicing personal disciplines
- learning holy obedience
- participating fully in community

As we take up our task as workers with Christ, we must also remember who we are as human beings. Our calling as servants is not to give away ourselves and our souls, but to give and receive instead the limitless love and mercy of God, our Creator, Redeemer, and Sustainer. Together we can unlearn and remember the spirituality we were given at birth. As we enter into the river of faith, we become new and rediscover the innocence we once knew:

Become a child, enter the kingdom.
Enter the kingdom, become a child.[7]

In the words of John Donne: "Batter my heart, three person'd God . . . and make me new."

Notes

Introduction

1. John Donne, *The Complete Poetry and Selected Prose of John Donne*, ed. Charles M. Coffin (New York: Modern Library, 1994), 252.

I. How Servanthood Affects the Soul

1. Rainer Maria Rilke, *Rilke's Book of Hours: Love Poems to God*, trans. Anita Barrows and Joanna Macy (New York: Riverhead Books, 1996), 70.
2. Geoffrey Hill, *Tenebrae* (Boston: Houghton Mifflin, 1979), 21.

2. Whose Power Is It Anyway?

1. Peg Thompson, *Finding Your Own Spiritual Path: An Everyday Guidebook* (San Francisco: HarperSanFrancisco, 1994), 182–83.
2. Frederick Herzog, "Diakonia in Modern Times: Eighteenth–Twentieth Centuries," in *Service in Christ: Essays Presented to Karl Barth on His 80th Birthday,* ed. James I. McCord and T. H. L. Parker (Grand Rapids: Eerdmans, 1966), 139.
3. Reinhold Niebuhr, *Moral Man and Immoral Society: A Study in Ethics and Politics* (New York: Scribner, 1960), 263–64.
4. William Stringfellow, *The Politics of Spirituality* (Philadelphia: Westminster Press, 1984), 45.
5. Ibid., 85.
6. Herzog, "Diakonia in Modern Times," 150.
7. Richard J. Foster and James Bryan Smith, eds., *Devotional Classics: Selected Readings for Individuals and Groups* (San Francisco: HarperSanFrancisco, 1993).
8. Eugene Peterson, *Spiritual Reading: An Annotated List,* June 1992, 9.

3. Entry Points and Ultimate Meaning

1. Reinhold Niebuhr, *The Contribution of Religion to Social Work* (New York: Columbia University Press, 1932), 71.
2. Robert K. Greenleaf, *Servant Leadership: A Journey into the Nature of Legitimate Power and Greatness* (New York/Mahwah: Paulist Press, 1991), 36.
3. John Ellerton, "O Grant Us, God, a Little Space," in *The New Century Hymnal* (Cleveland, Ohio: The Pilgrim Press, 1995), 516, alt.
4. Charles E. Hambrick-Stowe, *The Practice of Piety: Puritan Devotional Disciplines in 17th Century New England* (Chapel Hill: University of North Carolina Press, 1982), 77.
5. Malcolm Warford, *Our Several Callings: A Foundation Paper on Vocation as a Lifelong Issue for Education* (Cleveland, Ohio: The Division of Education and Publication, United Church Board for Homeland Ministries, 1990), 24.
6. Ibid., 24–25.
7. Ron Cole-Turner, *Hearing God's Call: A Resource Paper on Vocation as a Lifelong Issue for Education,* rev. ed. (Cleveland, Ohio: United Church Board for Homeland Ministries, 1994), 15.
8. Hambrick-Stowe, *The Practice of Piety,* 86.
9. John Shea, *The Hour of the Unexpected* (Allen, Tex.: Argus Communications, 1977), 90.
10. Cole-Turner, *Hearing God's Call,* 19.
11. Edward P. Wimberly, *Recalling Our Own Stories: Spiritual Renewal for Religious Caregivers* (San Francisco: Jossey-Bass, 1997).
12. Rilke, *Book of Hours,* 84.
13. Cynthia Robinson, "Ditches along the Way," *Spirit Unfolding,* from the Spiritual Development Network of the United Church of Christ, fall 1997, 3.
14. Rosie Johnson, in *Lifelink Focus* magazine, winter 1998, 13.
15. Laura Gron, in *Lifelink Focus* magazine, winter 1996, 15.
16. Amos Bradford, in *Lifelink Focus* magazine, summer 1995, 16.

17. Sanford Jaffe, in *Lifelink Focus* magazine, spring 1997, 14.

18. Michael Welker, *The Need for Church-Related Agencies to Address Ethical Issues in a Time of Declining Resources* (proceedings of the 1997 CHHSM Forum on Ethical Issues in Child and Family Services) (Cleveland, Ohio: United Church of Christ Council for Health and Human Service Ministries, 1997), 34.

4. Personal Discipline as a Fearsome Prospect

1. David Whyte, *The Heart Aroused: Poetry and the Preservation of the Soul in Corporate America* (New York: Currency Doubleday, 1994).

2. Dawn Gibeau, "Caring for Your Soul at Work," a review of David Whyte's *The Heart Aroused,* in *Praying* magazine, September–October 1997, 9–12.

3. Ibid., 11.

4. Ibid., 12.

5. John Shea, "Spirituality Outside the Churches," audiotape of lecture presented at Old St. Patrick's Church, Chicago (Chicago: ACTA Publications, 1996).

6. Wimberly, *Recalling Our Stories,* 10–11.

7. Richard Baxter, *The Reformed Pastor* (1655; reprint, London: SCM Press, 1956), 33–34.

8. Matthew Fox, *The Re-invention of Work: A New Vision of Livelihood for Our Time* (San Francisco: HarperSanFrancisco, 1995), 309–12.

9. Eden Theological Seminary faculty, *Spirituality: The Work of God the Holy Spirit in Our Lives,* ed. J. Clinton McCann Jr. (St. Louis: Eden Theological Seminary, 1990).

10. Shea, "Spirituality Outside the Churches."

11. Denise Levertov, *The Stream and the Sapphire: Selected Poems on Religious Themes* (New York: New Directions Publishing, 1997), 15–16.

12. Gibeau, "Caring for Your Soul at Work," 11.

13. Shea, "Spirituality Outside the Churches."

14. Hambrick-Stowe, *The Practice of Piety,* xv.

15. Peg Lodwick Jacobs, *Friends of God and Prophets: A Sampling of Spiritual Exercises for Compassion and Justice* (Cleveland, Ohio: Office for Church in Society, United Church of Christ, 1995).

16. Stringfellow, *The Politics of Spirituality,* 20.

17. Niebuhr, *The Contribution of Religion to Social Work,* 67.

18. Walter Wink, *Engaging the Powers* (Minneapolis: Fortress Press, 1982), 308.

19. Greenleaf, *Servant Leadership,* 7–48.

20. Reinhold Niebuhr, *The Irony of American History* (New York: Scribner, 1952), 63.

5. Obedience Lessons for Leaders

1. Greenleaf, *Servant Leadership,* 13–14.

2. Flora Slosson Wuellner, *Prayer, Stress and Our Inner Wounds* (Nashville: The Upper Room, 1985), 78.

3. Thomas Kelly, *A Testament of Devotion* (1941; reprint, New York: HarperCollins, 1992), 71.

4. Greenleaf, *Servant Leadership,* 26.

5. Ibid., 21.

6. Donne, *The Complete Poetry and Selected Prose of John Donne,* 252.

7. Charles Hambrick-Stowe, "Spiritual Exercises: Our Puritan Roots," *Newsletter of the Spiritual Development Network of the United Church of Christ,* November 30, 1984, 2.

8. Wendell Berry, *Collected Poems 1957–1982* (San Francisco: North Point Press, 1984), 65.

9. Bianco da Siena, "Come Forth, O Love Divine," trans. Richard F. Littledale, in *The New Century Hymnal,* 289, alt.

10. Greenleaf, *Servant Leadership,* 327.

6. Learning Interdependence in a World of Autonomy

1. Wuellner, Prayer, *Stress and Our Inner Wounds,* 85.
2. Marc Parent, *Turning Stones: My Days and Nights with Children at Risk* (New York: Harcourt, Brace, 1996), 341–49.
3. J. Mary Luti, "The Community of Faith," in *Habits of Faith,* ed. Leah F. Matthews (Cleveland, Ohio: The Division of Education and Publication, United Church Board for Homeland Ministries, 1997), 19.
4. Ibid., 24.
5. Greenleaf, *Servant Leadership,* 39.
6. Niebuhr, *The Contribution of Religion to Social Work,* 74–75.
7. In Jay A. Conger and Associates, *Spirit at Work: Discovering the Spirituality in Leadership* (San Francisco: Jossey-Bass, 1994), 100–131.
8. Ibid., 159.

7. Bringing Spirituality into a Life of Service

1. Thompson, *Finding Your Own Spiritual Path,* 158–59.
2. Chester P. Michael and Marie C. Norrisey, *Prayer and Temperament* (Charlottesville, Va.: Open Door, 1991).
3. James Bryan Smith, *A Spiritual Formation Workbook* (San Francisco: HarperSanFrancisco, 1993).
4. Robert McAfee Brown, *Spirituality and Liberation: Overcoming the Great Fallacy* (Philadelphia: Westminster Press, 1988), 47.
5. Wuellner, Prayer, *Stress and Our Inner Wounds,* 71–73.
6. Ibid., 89.
7. John Dominic Crossan, *The Essential Jesus: Original Sayings and Earliest Images* (San Francisco: HarperSanFrancisco, 1994), 45.

Selected Bibliography

Baxter, Richard. *The Reformed Pastor.* 1655. Reprint, London: SCM Press, 1956.

Berry, Wendell. *Collected Poems 1957–1982.* San Francisco: North Point Press, 1984.

Brown, Robert McAfee. *Spirituality and Liberation: Overcoming the Great Fallacy.* Philadelphia: Westminster Press, 1988.

Cole-Turner, Ron. *Hearing God's Call: A Resource Paper on Vocation as a Lifelong Issue for Education.* Rev. ed. Cleveland, Ohio: United Church Board for Homeland Ministries, 1994.

Conger, Jay A., and Associates. *Spirit at Work: Discovering the Spirituality in Leadership.* San Francisco: Jossey-Bass, 1994.

Crossan, John Dominic. *The Essential Jesus: Original Sayings and Earliest Images.* San Francisco: HarperSanFrancisco, 1994.

Donne, John. *The Complete Poetry and Selected Prose of John Donne.* Edited by Charles M. Coffin. New York: Modern Library, 1994.

Eden Theological Seminary faculty. *Spirituality: The Work of God the Holy Spirit in Our Lives.* Edited by J. Clinton McCann Jr. St. Louis: Eden Theological Seminary, 1990.

Foster, Richard J., and James Bryan Smith, eds. *Devotional Classics: Selected Readings for Individuals and Groups.* San Francisco: HarperSanFrancisco, 1993.

Fox, Matthew. *The Re-invention of Work: A New Vision of Livelihood for Our Time.* San Francisco: HarperSanFrancisco, 1995.

Greenleaf, Robert K. *Servant Leadership: A Journey into the Nature of Legitimate Power and Greatness.* New York/Mahwah: Paulist Press, 1991.

Hambrick-Stowe, Charles E. *The Practice of Piety: Puritan Devotional Disciplines in 17th Century New England.* Chapel Hill: University of North Carolina Press, 1982.

Hill, Geoffrey. *Tenebrae*. Boston: Houghton Mifflin, 1979.

Jacobs, Peg Lodwick. *Friends of God and Prophets: A Sampling of Spiritual Exercises for Compassion and Justice*. Cleveland, Ohio: Office for Church in Society, United Church of Christ, 1995.

Kelly, Thomas. *A Testament of Devotion*. 1941. Reprint, New York: HarperCollins, 1992.

Levertov, Denise. *The Stream and the Sapphire: Selected Poems on Religious Themes*. New York: New Directions Publishing, 1997.

Luti, J. Mary. "The Community of Faith." In *Habits of Faith,* edited by Leah F. Matthews. Cleveland, Ohio: The Division of Education and Publication, United Church Board for Homeland Ministries, 1997.

Michael, Chester P., and Marie C. Norrisey. *Prayer and Temperament*. Charlottesville, Va.: Open Door, 1991.

Niebuhr, Reinhold. *The Contribution of Religion to Social Work*. New York: Columbia University Press, 1932.

———. *The Irony of American History*. New York: Scribner, 1952.

———. *Moral Man and Immoral Society: A Study in Ethics and Politics*. New York: Scribner, 1960.

Parent, Marc. *Turning Stones: My Days and Nights with Children at Risk*. New York: Harcourt, Brace, 1996.

Rilke, Rainer Maria. *Rilke's Book of Hours: Love Poems to God*. Translated by Anita Barrows and Joanna Macy. New York: Riverhead Books, 1996.

Shea, John. *The Hour of the Unexpected*. Allen, Tex.: Argus Communications, 1977.

Smith, James Bryan. *A Spiritual Formation Workbook*. San Francisco: HarperSanFrancisco, 1993.

Stringfellow, William. *The Politics of Spirituality*. Philadelphia: Westminster Press, 1984.

Thompson, Peg. *Finding Your Own Spiritual Path: An Everyday Guidebook*. San Francisco: HarperSanFrancisco, 1994.

Warford, Malcolm. *Our Several Callings: A Foundation Paper on*

Vocation as a Lifelong Issue for Education. Cleveland, Ohio: The Division of Education and Publication, United Church Board for Homeland Ministries, 1990.

Whyte, David. *The Heart Aroused: Poetry and the Preservation of the Soul in Corporate America.* New York: Currency Doubleday, 1994.

Wimberly, Edward P. *Recalling Our Own Stories: Spiritual Renewal for Religious Caregivers.* San Francisco: Jossey-Bass, 1997.

Wink, Walter. *Engaging the Powers.* Minneapolis: Fortress Press, 1982.

Wuellner, Flora Slosson. *Prayer, Stress and Our Inner Wounds.* Nashville: The Upper Room, 1985.